STUDIES IN ENGLISH LITERATURE

Volume XXIV

THE COMEDY

OF

SIR WILLIAM DAVENANT

by

HOWARD S. COLLINS

Cuttington College, Liberia

1967

MOUTON

THE HAGUE · PARIS

For my mother and father

PREFACE

The man with a general interest in seventeenth-century letters will probably be aware of Sir William Davenant as a somewhat opportunistic courtier who attempted to aggrandize himself by circulating the story that Shakespeare was his father. The college student with a more specialized study of the period probably concerns himself with Davenant as the man who introduced "opera" to England and fathered what was to become known as heroic drama. In this work I propose to ignore the first point; though intriguing, to be sure, still it should never have warranted the excess of attention it has received. As for the second point, certainly of importance, it has already been examined with housewifely thoroughness. Rather I wish to make a critical study of Sir William Davenant's dramaturgic treatment of the Comic Spirit.

Davenant was the only important playwright to span the Stuart, Caroline, Interregnum, and Restoration periods. During this time remarkable changes in the treatment of dramatic comedy were to be noted, and, as to be expected of a man who adjusted so well to the varying political and social fortunes of the time, Davenant reflected the changing mode. Yet of his concern with the Comic Spirit, little of worth has been written. Most critics up to the time of A. W. Ward did little more than mention that Davenant had written comedies. Ward showed more interest for he valued Davenant as a chief link between the Elizabethan and Restoration drama. Still he, too, is often condescending in his appraisal, and at times he is curiously obtuse, a failing that is to be noted in the statement, "but of the humor in which Fletcher abounded,

Davenant seems to me to possess little or nothing". Again, later, his own inability to recognize rightly a play's relation to its time is expressed in the curiously cavalier remark, "The comedy of *The Wits* . . . seems to me to have been greatly overvalued." Such pronouncements by such an authority have had their effect: no one reads Davenant today – except for *The Siege of Rhodes* – but all who have heard of him are quick to claim that he is tedious.

The first modern scholar to assess this dramatist's worth was Leslie Hotson in his *The Commonwealth and Restoration Stage* (1928), which grew out of his unpublished Harvard dissertation, "Sir William Davenant, and the Commonwealth Stage" (1923). Both works are concerned with Davenant as a producer and theatrical innovator, not with an internal study of his drama. In 1935, Alfred Harbage published his research biography and critical reevaluation, titled *Sir William Davenant, Poet Venturer, 1606-1668*. In this very readable work Harbage includes a short chapter on Davenant's treatment of comedy, but outside of witnessing that a definite talent in that line existed, there is no intensive or extensive study of its dramaturgic treatment. Three years later Arthur Nethercot's *Sir William D'Avenant, Poet Laureate and Playwright Manager* appeared, which is of value solely for its more scholarly accumulation of biographical details. Then, too, in Montague Summers' *The Playhouse of Pepys* (1935) there is a brief but informative chapter on various performances and casts of individual plays by Davenant. No other work of value on this dramatist exists, and certainly none that seriously treats this playwright's concern for the comic.

In this examination of Davenant, I propose to reveal him as a creator of various forms of dramatic comedy, of humors, satire, manners, and even burlesque which, incidentally, Davenant introduced to the Restoration stage, thereby establishing a theatrical mode of continuing interest. I propose to reveal Davenant as a playwright who employed a not inconsiderable talent to portray the types of comedy that were then favored, and thus aided in transporting the valued traditions of one age of comedy across the gap of two decades into a period of significantly more brilliant comedy. To succeed in this task will be to restore Davenant to a position no higher than he deserves, but certainly more lofty than that which he could boast of now.

Of the several obligations which I have incurred during my study, I must acknowledge first the late professor of English at Brown University, Mr. Robert Gale Noyes. His patience and tact will long be remembered. A more considerate mentor a student could not have.

For his sense of humor, a desired quality when a book is in the process of being written, Professor John Gearey of New York University was indispensable.

To my several friends at Ohio's Oberlin College and Liberia's Cuttington College, too numerous to name here, I also owe thanks for their encouraging support.

Suakoko, Liberia   *H. S. C.*

TABLE OF CONTENTS

I

CAREER, LITERARY AND OTHERWISE

If we may accept legend, and legend usually has some basis in fact, Sir William Davenant's literary baptism was foreshadowed auspiciously by his physical baptism. For it is said that on March 3, 1606, at the church of St. Martin's in Oxford, William Shakespeare himself acted as chief sponsor for this future Laureate of England.[1] Be it true or not, Davenant, all his life, was to flatter himself with the thought that he was a "literary son" of the great dramatist.

William Davenant's formative years do not demand detailed attention. His home life might be considered respectably bourgeois. In what was probably the liveliest university town in the world, John Davenant, his father, was a successful vintner. There, in back of the tavern, Jane Davenant reared her seven children, keenly desirous of pressing every opportunity that the advantageous town-and-gown relationship might offer her growing family.

Unfortunately, William, unlike his older brothers, showed little

---

[1] The legend of Shakespeare being Davenant's godfather with its accompanying scandalous suggestions has been noted in several sources. Probably John Aubrey did most to circulate this story. See *Aubrey's Brief Lives*, ed. Oliver Lawson Dick (London, 1950), p. 85. William Oldys, Alexander Pope, and John Taylor, the "Water Poet", are other names involved in its telling and retelling, by no means to their credit. Of his recent biographers only Alfred Harbage seems to discredit the tales. Arthur Nethercot would like to believe it simply because he finds it a tantalizing tidbit, and Montague Summers in *The Playhouse of Pepys* (London, 1935), p. 5, writes "... although myself I see no reason at all why the story may not be accepted." Since it is unlikely that the truth will ever be known, the reader can, with equal justification, accept either view.

inclination towards a University education. Perhaps if he had, his later ambition towards a literary career would have been less frustrated. In any case, before his parents died in 1622, it was clear that other means of livelihood must be secured for a boy whose very restlessness and lack of inner direction might prove an obstacle to himself and the other Davenant heirs. Thus it is not surprising that the father's will stipulated that William was to "be put to prentice to some good merchant of London or other tradesman".[2] In doing so he spurred his son's departure from humdrum respectability towards a world that would shape more surely the way to fame.[3]

An ambitious lad could hardly learn more swiftly how to function in court life than through employment as a page in an aristocratic household. As such in the service of the arrogant and

---

[2]   Arthur Acheson, *Shakespeare's Sonnet Story 1592-1598* (London, 1922). See the "Will of John Davenant (of Oxford)", pp. 658-663.

[3]   *Critical Essays of the Seventeenth Century*, ed. Joel E. Spingarn (Oxford, 1908-1909), pp. 29-30. In his "Preface to Gondibert", Davenant admits that his reason for writing was a desire for fame: "Men are chiefly provok'd to the toyl of compiling Books by love of Fame, and often by officiousness of Conscience, but seldom with expectation of Riches; for those that spend time in writing to instruct others may finde leasure to inform themselves how mean the provisions are which busy and studious minds can make for their own sedentary bodies: And learned men, to whom the rest of the world are but Infants, have the same foolish affection in nourishing others minds as Pellicans in feeding their young, which is at the expence of the very subsistance of Life. 'Tis then apparent they proceed by the instigation of Fame or Conscience; and I believe many are persuaded by the first (of which I am One) and some are commanded by the second. Nor is the desire of Fame so vain as divers have rigidly imagin'd, Fame being, when belonging to the Living, that which is more gravely call'd a steady and necessary reputation, and without it hereditary Power or acquir'd greatness can never quietly govern the World. 'Tis of the dead a musical glory, in which God, the author of excellent goodness, vouchsafes to take a continual share: For the remember'd vertues of great men are chiefly such of his works, mention'd by King David, as perpetually praise him; and the good fame of the Dead prevails by example much more than the reputation of the Living, because the later is alwayes suspected by our Envy, but the other is cheerfully allow'd and religiously admir'd; for Admiration, whose Eyes are ever weak, stands still and at gaze upon great things acted far off, but when they are neer, walks slightly away as from familiar objects. Fame is to our Sons a solid Inheritance, and not unuseful to remote Posterity; and to our Reason, 'tis the first though but a little taste of Eternity."

aging Duchess of Richmond, Davenant became acquainted with a social brilliance that few courtiers could equal. But such an education was of short duration. The Duke of Richmond died in 1624, leaving his wife in reduced circumstances. Davenant was inevitably one of her "small economies". Lack of employment, however, was no immediate hardship, for about this time Davenant received the £150 stipulated in his father's legacy. Supported by such, he undertook to get married. Concerning this first wife, Mary, little is known, except that she bore two children and then died before they were grown. Before long Davenant entered into the service of Fulke Greville, the onetime companion of Philip Sidney. Undoubtedly association with a man who had belonged to the Pembroke circle would be of inspiring influence to one with literary aims. In fact, it was during this time that Davenant was to try his hand at writing tragedies. But in 1628 Greville was murdered by a dissatisfied servant, and once more Davenant was without occupation.

Having authored two tragedies, one a closet piece called *Albovine* and the other, *The Cruel Brother*, which reached the theatre in performance, Davenant had been sufficiently encouraged not to forsake his goal. Still he had to find a new patron. His first step was to seek contacts at the Inns of Court. Taking lodging there he soon met scions of the most illustrious families. Fraternizing with them, indulging in the frenzied pleasures they too often enjoyed, must have consumed many precious hours of a poet's time, and yet he managed to continue playwriting. *The Siege* appeared in 1629, soon followed by *The Just Italian*. Youth was on his side. By pleasing others as well as pleasing himself, Davenant was forcing his wedge into fashionable circles. But his youth was also to lead him into pranks that were to be severely regretted. According to Aubrey, it was a "black, handsome wench that lay in Axe-yard, Westminster" that favored the poet with venereal disease. In any case, at the time Davenant was on a brief expedition with Buckingham's army, and like many foolish young men in military service he was more eager than prudent in choosing his female company. Treatment for the Grand Pox, as it was then called, required mercury. Unwisely administered its results

could be most unfortunate. Davenant's reminder of such a
ravaging cure was a nose so mulitated that it was to be an object
of scorn, or pity, but usually the former, for the rest of his life.
Then hardly was this affliction mended when his rash temper
caused him to wound an ostler fatally. Protection from the law he
found in Holland, and there he remained until hot tempers at home
had been quenched and his own volatile spirits somewhat sobered.
In 1633 Davenant was again in London where he was to find his
patron at the King's Court.

His first comedy, *The Wits*, brought him to the attention of
Charles I because of a dispute over its suitability for licensing.
The matter settled, the play was "well likt" at court, and its author
was in time commissioned to flatter the Queen's latest craze.
Henrietta Maria, schooled as a girl under the influence of the
Hôtel de Rambouillet, having digested thoroughly the precious
L'Astrée of Honoré d'Urfé, was determined to bring Platonic
Love to her husband's somewhat wayward court. How better and
more entertainingly could she do it than presentation through
theatricals? Jonson, having refused to work with Inigo Jones, and
the latter being utterly indispensable for his gorgeous scenic effects, Davenant was recruited to fulfill the subsidiary role. For the
writer of *The Wits*, a masque celebrating an unconsummated relationship between the sexes was indeed no easy commission. That
his *The Temple of Love* pleased is evident in that the Queen
honored the poet with her livery.

Other works on the same topic were to follow. *Love and
Honour*, a tragi-comedy, in its very title hailed a theme that was
to have great vogue on the stage. *The Platonick Lovers* approaches
it again as a tragi-comedy, though veering close to satire. *The
Triumphs of the Prince D'Amour*, a masque, presented the same
idea in lavish production in honor of the visiting Palatine princes.
Yet none of these works can begin to equal in quality the one play
that is an exception to those which Davenant was writing at this
time. *News from Plymouth*, a roistering comedy, was his only early
work not written for an aristocratic private audience. Presented
at the plebeian Globe, it catered to a more basic appreciation of
comedy, and in doing so it has more right to be termed comic.

Until the Interregnum Davenant's social, financial, and literary successes were to continue. It would be unfair to denounce Davenant as a mere court flunkey, yet it cannot be denied that he was willing to dazzle his benefactors at their request. *Britannia Triumphans* and *Luminalia* were two masques of magnificent splendor and sometimes soporific rhetoric. *Salmacida Spolia* even allowed for the Queen herself, obviously pregnant, to take part in the rather dangerous if not ridiculous role of being hoisted by a machine in order to make an entrance as if descending from a cloud. *The Unfortunate Lovers* was another Italianate tragedy, while *The Fair Favorite* foreshadowed the approaching heroic drama, delicately diluted with strains of sentimentality. *The Distresses* revealed the Spanish influence that was to become so prevalent among dramatists in the decades to come. Considering this output, it is not surprising that Charles should deem Davenant worthy of being Jonson's successor. Though he was never to have the title of Poet Laureate officially by letters patent, still it was obvious to his contemporaries that the king's financial grant in 1638 was sufficiently significant.

From 1640 to 1656 the new Laureate was not to have a play produced. Political events prevented any such frivolity. Nor would Davenant, loyal as he was, care to shirk his more important responsibilities to the ousted Crown.

It would be impossible in a brief biographical sketch to enumerate the intrigues involving Davenant. He was a Royalist, sincerely so, and as such supported his patron with unswerving devotion. Before attending the Queen to France in February, 1642, he had already been apprehended for his political contrivances and barely averted execution for high treason. On the Continent and again at home he served under William Cavendish, Earl of Newcastle, as Lieutenant-general of the ordnance. For one who only five years before had been a mere "ancient", he advanced swiftly. But his honor was to be still magnified. At the siege of Gloucester, Charles I dubbed his faithful servant a knight. Such recognition was warranted. As the royal forces continued to disintegrate and the monarch's position became increasingly perilous, Davenant entered upon his most desperate mission. The

Queen and her advisers believed the King could save himself only
by abjuring Episcopacy and in uniting with the Scottish and English Presbyterians against the English Independents and anti-
monarchists. As special envoy in this cause, Davenant pleaded
with expected eloquence. Needless to say, to the King's credit, the
poet failed. Though the King was later to weaken and offer con-
cessions equal to Davenant's prpoosal, it was then too late. His
doom was fixed. In 1649 the Cavalier cause was lost when Charles
was beheaded at Whitehall.

Tedious exile was to continue, during which Davenant returned
to his vocation and began work on what would become the un-
finished epic *Gondibert*. Engrossed as he was, he was evidently
urged to put it aside and enter upon a more exciting venture. For
in the early months of 1650 he was making preparations to sail to
America in order to become the new Governor of Maryland. But
his plan was foiled. Hardly had he set sail than some parliamen-
tary ships appeared. Taken prisoner he spent the entire summer in
Cowes Castle and then was moved to the Tower. Pending trial he
whiled away his hours in working on his epic, but as to how well
he could concentrate, it would be difficult to judge. Certainly the
charges against him were serious. Yet they were never pressed. As
to the exact circumstances surrounding the Council of State's
signed order for his release, no one seems to know. Of the several
surmises, the most appealing, though there is no supporting evidence, is that Milton himself intervened in his behalf. Probably
what did happen was simply that Parliament was of a calmer
temper, becoming more objective in its definition of treason. After
two and a half years of imprisonment, two of them spent in the
Tower, Davenant was freed on the promise that he would remain
in London.

Literature was not his immediate goal upon securing freedom.
Rather, his wife being dead, he married the widow of the physician who had cured his disfiguring malady some twenty years
earlier. Whether or not this marriage was an act of gratitude because she had provided his bail is unknown. In any case this move
was not for a fortune, since soon afterwards he was again in prison, hounded by creditors. Fortunately, the matter was temporarily

solved and Davenant was released. Still, in a very few months he again found himself a widower with the sole responsibility of four stepsons. This time he returned to his craft and restored a semi-legitimate theatre to England.

Aided by the dowry of his third wife, a French widow, he secured rights to Rutland House, once a nobleman's mansion. Here he intended to present before an invited public, for a slight fee, entertainments of a musical and/or moral order. Carefully avoiding the terminology of theatre, he borrowed the foreign word "opera", thus hoping to avert any hostility. The first work presented was titled *The First Dayes Entertainment at Rutland House, by Declamations and Musick: after the manner of the Ancients.* Preserved state papers show that a government spy was present, but evidently this "opera" must have seemed harmless for such entertainments continued to flourish. Three months later, still unmolested, Davenant produced *The Siege of Rhodes*, one of the milestones in our drama. Emboldened by the success both of it and revivals of his earlier dramas, he dared to transfer his presentations to the more commodious Cockpit in Drury-Lane. Here, capitalizing on contemporary hatred of Spain, he produced a mish-mash of theatrical forms titled *The Cruelty of the Spaniards in Peru*, and then followed it with the episodic *The History of Sir Francis Drake.* By eschewing obvious dramatic scenes and larding it heavily with music and dancing, he managed to avoid the fatal stigma of producing a "stage play". However, his luck could not last. Fears of a counter-revolution were rife, and of the three thousand Royalists in London, all of whom were distrusted, Davenant was prominent. Briefly imprisoned, his theatre closed, having suffered years of insecurity, he must have been deeply relieved when the Rump Parliament finally dissolved and England prepared for the return of her monarchy.

With the Restoration, Davenant's prospects improved. In age and temperament he was not too compatible with Charles II's rowdy court, but, out of respect for his past services, he was rewarded with the managership of the Duke's Playhouse, one of the two licensed theatres. The last eight years of his life were devoted to this cause. Training and directing his actors and actresses, settling quarrels, and fighting lawsuits filled his days. There was little time left for writing, and what there was of it revealed a diminishing of inspiration. *A Playhouse to be Let*, compounded of some Commonwealth pieces, an adaptation from the French, and a broad burlesque, was his most original offering. Otherwise he relied on translations and adaptations. His "godfather", Shakespeare, he attempted to present according to prevailing tastes, and these tastes alone should be blamed for what resulted. *The Law Against Lovers* was a combination of *Measure for Measure* and *Much Ado About Nothing*. *The Rivals* was based on *The Two Noble Kinsmen*, and both *Macbeth* and *The Tempest* received labored attention. His last effort, *The Man's the Master*, based on a French play, required a second visit of Pepys before that illustrious diarist could feel satisfied. And perhaps his final judgment was somewhat tempered by the recent death of the Poet Laureate.

On April 7, 1668, Samuel Pepys was absorbed in the gossip of the town when news was brought of Davenant's death. Two days later he watched the corpse being carried to Westminster Abbey, where John Aubrey was an invited guest:

I was at his funerall. He had a coffin of Walnutt-tree; Sir John Denham sayd 'twas the finest coffin that ever he saw. His body was carried in a Herse from the Play-house to Westminster-abbey, where, at the great West dore, he was received by the Singingman and Choristers, who sang the Service of the Church (I am the Resurrection, etc.) to his Grave, which is in the South crosse aisle, on which, on a paving stone of marble, is writt, in imitation of that on Ben Johnson: *O rare Sir Will. Davenant.*[4]

---

[4] *Aubrey's Brief Lives*, p. 88.

II

COMEDY IN THE SEVENTEENTH CENTURY

The first function of the Comic Spirit is to make man laugh.[1] It may be a full-throated guffaw, it may be a smile, it may only be a pleasant elation of the thought processes that evokes no physical manifestation whatsoever, but foremost is its desire to please man's sense of mirth. To attempt to define the Comic Spirit without keeping this seemingly obvious explanation in mind, and it has been done, is as patently ridiculous as defining tragedy without concern for its necessary element of terror. The Comic Spirit, working in its most pleasurable fashion, brings man unbounded joy, rich and heady. At its least attractive, it subjects one to the ambivalent though coruscating effects of scorn. Between these two poles, at varying positions, can be found terms defining other faces of the elusive Muse: Humor, Irony, Satire, Sarcasm, and Wit. In all, even the most destructive in intent, the guiding route is on a ray of laughter.

The answer for why man laughs has intrigued the philosophers from Plato to Bergson. Plato asserted that pleasure is evoked as an emotional release when the power of fate suddenly is realized as not being a power at all but only the semblance of power.[2] It is impotence masquerading as fate. Thus fear, when removed, is replaced by the relief of pleasure, and so laughter results. Aristotle in the *Poetics* claims that it is caused by "some defect or ugliness,

---

[1] The term "Comic Spirit" as such was given its present widespread use as a result of George Meredith's *Essay on Comedy*.
[2] Plato, *Philebus*, chapters 30-50. See *Philebus and Epinomis*, trans. A. E. Taylor (London, 1956), pp. 132-172.

which is not painful or destructive",[3] and the obvious example of
this is the comic mask, distorted yet delighting. In the *Rhetoric* he
suggests that it is the result of a deceived expectation.[4] Alhough
both explanations, when combined, would restate the idea of
Plato, when separated they confuse. This conflict in interpretation
has persisted until today. Hobbes in his *Discourse on Human
Nature* would seem to agree with the *Poetics* when he states that
"the passion of laughter is nothing else but sudden glory arising
from a sudden conception of some eminency in ourselves, by comparison with the infirmity of others, or with our own formerly".[5]
And to be sure much laughter, often but not necessarily of an unkind variety, would support the truth of such a theory. Yet another type of laugh, and one more commonly noted in relation to
our sunnier comedies, is better explained by Emmanuel Kant:
"Laughter is an affection arising from the sudden transformation
of a strained expectation into nothing." [6] In the late nineteenth
century George Meredith became more specific:

Man's future upon earth does not attract it; their honesty and shape-
liness in the present does; and whenever they wax out of proportion,
overblown, affected, pretentious, bombastical, hypocritical, pedantic,
fantastically delicate; whenever it sees them self-deceived or hoodwinked, given to run riot in idolatries, drifting into vanities, con-
gregating in absurdities, planning short-sightedly, plotting dementedly;
whenever they offered sound reason, fair justice; are false in humility
or mined with conceit, individually, or in the bulk – the Spirit overhead will look humanely malign and cast an oblique light on them,
followed by volleys of silvery laughter. This is the Comic Spirit.[7]

Considering such statements, and they are representative of what
the philosophers have pronounced, one is ultimately impressed by

[3]   Aristotle, *Poetics*, chapter 5. See *Aristotle on the Art of Poetry*, ed.
Lane Cooper (New York, 1913), pp. 14-16.
[4]   Aristotle, *Rhetoric*, Bk. I, Ch. xii. See *The Rhetoric of Aristotle*, trans.
J. E. C. Welldon (London, 1886), pp. 85-92.
[5]   Thomas Hobbes, *Discourse on Human Nature*, in *The English Works
of Thomas Hobbes of Malmesbury* (London, 1840), IV, pp. 45-46.
[6]   *Kant's Critique of Aesthetic Judgment*, trans. James Creed Meredith
(Oxford, 1911), p. 199.
[7]   George Meredith, *An Essay on Comedy and the Uses of the Comic
Spirit*, ed. Lane Cooper (New York, 1918), pp. 83-84.

the suggestion implicit in all their various statements that laughter is not entirely and purely a happy act. Plato understood this. In the *Philebus*, through the mouth of Socrates, he claims that at a comedy the soul experiences a blending of pleasure and pain.[8] Regardless of their disagreement as to what phenomenon exists to produce laughter, the authorities would seem to agree, if not with equal conviction, that the motivating principle is pleasure/pain. This double-edged principle is directly linked to a Comic Spirit that is, if anything, critical. In essence the Comic Spirit is intellect – emotion is mere ramification – and being so its discerning eye seeks the contrast between man's true position and man's ideal position in the universe. From the proverbial gentleman who slipped on the banana peel to Oscar Wilde's Algernon with his absurd obsession for cucumber sandwiches, the Comic Spirit always detects an element of incongruity in the human conflict. Between what man pretends himself to be, whether in his relationship with other human beings or in his relationship to his milieu, and the reality of what actually exists lies the incongruity. This is apparent to the mind, causing pain. Instinctively man would wince were it not for another instinct, that which seeks relief from pain. This relief, still a mental act, is to laugh and feel pleasure. If he does not laugh, but rather contemplates the incongruity, dwelling on it emotionally, he ceases to see the amusing aspect and feels the pity. Horace Walpole explained this proximity of tears and laughter in his well-known maxim, "This world is a comedy to those that think, a tragedy to those that feel." [9] Therefore if tears are to be avoided, the pleasure part of the principle must be more powerful in its effect than the pain, and this pleasure is assisted by the very sociability that characterizes comedy.

Though tragedy and comedy are based on the same theme, the disparity between the real and ideal in human life, tragedy is a private affair, felt in the heart, and comedy is public, entertaining the intellect. The Comic Spirit desires group-mentality. As Bergson

---

[8]   Plato, *Philebus*, chapter 48, in *Philebus and Epinomis*, pp. 166-168.
[9]   Horace Walpole, "Letter to Countess of Upper Ossory, August 16, 1776", in *The Letters of Horace Walpole Fourth Earl of Oxford*, ed. Mrs. Paget Toynbee (Oxford, 1904), IX, p. 403.

has noted, the intelligence to which the comic appeals must always be kept in touch with other intelligences.[10] A group of people provides a consciousness of kind that assists the spectator in seeing the comic and ignoring the tragic. Anyone who has ever sat alone in an empty theatre at a comedy will attest to the increase of pain and decrease of pleasure that the performance provides. With a very slight adjustment of the receptive faculties, what would otherwise in a crowd seem quite hilarious can become rather terrifying. For this proper adjustment of the receptive faculties, a group of people is necessary. At such a time man is aware of his kinship to other human beings, who are also noting the irrationalities of human existence in which all are included. Immediately upon the pang of recognizing our own foibles to be as serious as another's comes the comfort of knowing that others are no better. Such understanding evokes the risible, lightening the conscious burden, and so man laughs.

If comedy is social, it follows naturally that its most effective habitat is the stage. Here in the dramatization of human behavior there are several causes to provoke a laugh: Physical Attributes of Characters; Personality of Characters; Situations Involving Characters; Manners being practised; Words spoken in Dialogue, and particularly its important branch called Wit; and Satire. In a good comedy several of them would work together. In what one might call "pure comedy", some may be undesirable, such as satire. But in this analysis there is no concern for so-called "pure comedy". That which produces an elation of the mental faculties, tending towards laughter, is our sole criterion for comedy. And in the light of this criterion, it is our intent to discuss Davenant's treatment of the Comic Spirit.[11]

---

[10]   Henri Bergson, *Laughter; an Essay on the Meaning of the Comic*, auth. trans. by Cloudsley Brereton and Fred Rothwell (New York, 1912), p. 5.
[11]   Other secondary works on comedy that have been considered helpful are: Louis Cazamian, *The Development of English Humor, Parts I and II* (Durham, 1952); J. Feibleman, *In Praise of Comedy* (New York, 1939); J. Y. T. Greig, *The Psychology of Laughter and Comedy* (New York, 1923); Louis Kronenberger, *The Thread of Laughter* (New York, 1952); Anthony M. Ludovici, *The Secret of Laughter* (London, 1932); Henry Ten

Before studying separately the works of Davenant, it would be helpful to note the various genres of dramatic comedy that were popularly presented in the seventeenth century. By discussing each type separately, by referring to notable examples of such for purposes of clarifying illustration, it will be more immediately pictured what kinds of comedy Davenant favored. The three common categories, all of which had their influence on this dramatist, were the comedy of intrigues, the comedy of humors, and the comedy of manners.

The comedy of intrigue in its clearest definition would refer to that comedy which is based on Spanish comedies of intrigue.[12] Since *Calisto and Melibea*, an adaptation of a Spanish romance, probably by Fernando de Rojas,[13] the Spanish influence had been felt on English drama. Like other Jacobean dramatists Beaumont and Fletcher borrowed occasionally. Some seventeen or more of the plays listed in their combined folio are derived from Spanish sources, according to Montague Summers.[14] But it was not until the Restoration that the contribution of the Spanish theatre to English comedy warranted serious attention. From 1660 to 1670, with Calderon as the most favored figure of interest, followed by Lope de Vega, Guillen de Castro, Alarcón, Zorilla, and Moretto, Spanish plots of intrigue fascinated the brilliant courtly audiences. Sir Walter Scott describes the reason for the attraction in that the English preferred "the Spanish comedy with its bustle, machinery, disguise and complicated intrigue", and were entertained by "its adventures, surprises, rencounters, mistakes, disguises, and escapes, all easily accomplished by the intervention of sliding panels, closets, veils, masques, large cloaks, and dark lanthorns".[15]

Eyck Perry, *Masters of Dramatic Comedy and their Social Themes* (Cambridge, Mass., 1939); Willard Smith, *The Nature of Comedy* (Boston, 1930).
[12]   There is an early analysis of this Spanish influence that is written in German, which is still of value: Arthur Ludwig Stiefel, "Die Nachahmung spanischer Komödien in England unter den ersten Stuarts", *Romanische Forschungen* (Erlangen, 1890), V.
[13]   Montague Summers, "Introduction" to Sir Samuel Tuke's *The Adventure of Five Hours*, ed. H. Van Thal (London, no date), p. xiv.
[14]   Page xvii.
[15]   Sir Walter Scott, "Life of John Dryden", in *The Works of John Dryden* (London, 1808), I, pp. 74-75.

This type of comedy influenced Dryden considerably, and Mrs. Aphra Behn's literary career would have been hard pressed without such sources. But the most sensational translation from the Spanish was surely Sir Samuel Tuke's *The Adventures of Five Hours.*[16] When produced in January, 1662-3, its reception was extraordinary. Downes states that it "took Successively 13 Days together, no other play intervening",[17] certainly a "long run" for that age. John Evelyn thought "the plot was incomparable . . .",[18] whereas Samuel Pepys saw the play four times prior to 1670, read it twice, and was enthusiastic as to its merits.[19] Had Charles II not suggested the feasibility of this translation to Tuke, it is quite likely that this particular species would not have had such a violent theatrical vogue.

A brief glance at this tightly-constructed play reveals it as telling a bustling tale that combines the time-honored themes of love, honor, and revenge. A brother arranges to have his sister marry a soldier she does not love, and by proxy too, in order to prevent her from marrying a man who he thinks loves another woman. Unfortunately, to his ignorance, the soldier loves this other woman, having at one time rescued her. These misunderstandings are merely the beginning of situations which, to the unwary spectator, become hopelessly muddled. A duel is fought, a man dies, and another goes into hiding. Gallants swear allegiance to aid each other, little knowing the dire consequences that are enjoined upon them. A lady is abducted, her captor mistaking her identity. Another maiden, fearing her brother's vengeance for her having sullied the family honor, resolves to escape. Later the hero is faced with the unhappy demand of choosing between loyalty to love and loyalty to his friend. Eventually all these complications are

---

[16]   Allison Gaw, "Tuke's *Adventures of Five Hours*, in Relation to the 'Spanish Plot' and to John Dryden", *Studies in English Drama*, ed. Allison Gaw (Baltimore, 1917), p. 59.

[17]   John Downes, *Roscius Anglicanus*, ed. Montague Summers (London, no date), pp. 22-23.

[18]   John Evelyn, *The Diary of John Evelyn, Esq., F.R.S. from 1641 to 1705-6*, ed. William Bray (London, no date), p. 292.

[19]   Gaw, p. 13.

disentangled, however, and the events end abruptly in apparent happiness. Generally these busy proceedings are gravely presented, but at times the servants intrude with some ludicrous capers. At no time does there seem to be an opportunity for character development, the various ladies and gentlemen being almost undifferentiated as individuals. Throughout its entire traffic on the stage, the emphasis is on plot.

Important as this Spanish influence was on the English comedy of intrigue, it would be erroneous to suppose that it was the only influence on this genre. Comedy in England had long had an aspect which was developing towards it. The Latin comedies presented at the universities are a definite source. See the *Menaechmi* of Plautus as a vivid example. Later Italian comedies also maintained the complicated web of intrigue, and to these Shakespeare, like others, was attracted. *Twelfth Night* was one of the results. In fact all of Shakespeare's romantic comedies, to a varying degree, of course, contain elements of intrigue. The same may be claimed for the comedies of Chapman, Jonson, Marston, and Middleton. If plot interest was not the sole interest in some of these comedies, it was only because their dramatists had a more comprehensive vision of the possibilities of comic drama. And it is quite possible that if a careful study were made, one might discover that the eventual disintegration of intrigue comedy into boisterous farce could be attributed largely to these strains of intrigue in comedy that were already existing on the English boards long before the Spanish plots had any real impact.

Just as it may seem arbitrary to isolate comedy of intrigue from other types of comic drama, so is it arbitrary to isolate the comedy of humors, for both are frequently found in comedies that are generally classified otherwise. For instance, both had a great part in the structure of the Restoration comedy of manners. And yet, if the features of such types are to be revealed in bold relief, it is necessary for purposes of study to isolate these genres.

When one thinks of the comedy of humors, one thinks of Ben Jonson, and probably his comedy *Every Man in His Humour,* perhaps even his later *Every Man Out of His Humour.* In the Induction of this latter play, wherein his critical theories are most slavishly put to the test, he explained his conception of comic caricature:

> As when some one peculiar quality
> Doth so possess a man, that it doth draw
> All his affects, his spirits, and his powers,
> In their conflictions all to run one way,
> This may be said to be a humour.

Thus, to him, in accordance with prevailing Elizabethan psychology, most men were suffering from any one of several disordered mental states in which all the forces of the individual personality are channeled by a dominating "humor". When all the humors come to balance harmoniously in the individual, as they usually do at the conclusion of such a comedy, then and only then can the ideal norm of human behavior be attained. As a playwright it was his duty, thought Jonson, to expose the human weaknesses resulting from such a controlling humor. To do this he resorted to an exaggeration of character traits, namely caricature.

In *Every Man in His Humour*, wherein Jonson wishes to "sport with human follies not with crimes", the spectator meets several "humorous" characters. Edward Knowell, Senior, an overly-anxious father, suspecting his son of frittering away his time in writing poetry and fraternizing with a charming gentleman playboy, determines some mild parental chastisement. The son, apprised of his father's knowledge, accepts the situation in good spirits. Meanwhile he consorts with his cousin Stephen, a wealthy country gull who wants to become a city gentleman, and Master Matthew, a foolish city gull who fancies himself a poet. The latter admires one Captain Bobadill, a military braggart of a somewhat saturnine disposition. This plot is further elaborated, and fortunately so, by Kitely, a rich merchant who has lately married and is inordinately jealous of his wife, forever fearful of being made a cuckold. Likewise Dame Kitely is equally suspicious of her spouse. Complications involving the above characters are generally effected by Brainworm, a man-servant who delights in mischief and ingenuity. All these characters in psychological conception are rigidly limited. Each has his own *idée fixe*, and each nurses it with obsession. Around his particular vice the comedy of his personality revolves. As a result these people do not have integral relations with others or with their environment. Rather the dramatist has deliberately imposed upon them an oversimplified character that will not act with but instead blunders against another constricted character. To be sure, they are delineated consistently and boldly, sometimes tediously so, but they lack the complexity and the common sense of real people. Nevertheless, the very distinctness of such types, the eccentricities of whom are displayed with a sharp liveliness, is often enormously comic. Certainly one would understand how such a theory of comedy can lend itself so snugly to satire.

Though this comedy of humors under Jonson's aegis often appears thoroughly English, particularly in setting, mood, and dialogue, the conception of it was not native to England. Plautus was the principal source. From the Roman comedy Jonson adopted the deceived father and sporting son, the shrewd servant, the vainglorious captain, and the gull, all stereotypes. Indeed, many of the situations in the comedy were stock situations in both Plautus and Terence. Native English comedy also provides an ancestor to this theory, in its own time in debt to the Romans. Surely the method of the old morality plays was similar to that of humor comedy in the abstract qualities that were clothed as men. The moralities as well applied this method in their criticism of a frail society. Less than a century later Shakespeare's Malvolio, Jaques, and Osric, to name only a few, are representative of such a conception of characterization. They exist solely to illustrate, in the interest of comedy, the Elizabethan belief concerning the humors that govern man's makeup. But it was chiefly Jonson who used this psychology to construct a kind of comedy that was to be distinctly English and profoundly influential. All his contemporary comic dramatists were affected to some degree. Nor was the comedy of humors to be forgotten with the Restoration. Scarcely a comedy of manners exists that does not feel the stamp of Jonson's genius, particularly in its stress on character. So popular did it remain that a lesser dramatist like Thomas Shadwell was to be able at the end of the century to have a successful career writing comedies that belonged almost completely to Jonson's mold. The importance of this kind of comedy helped to raise the comic form to a loftier and more seriously considered position in English drama; for this, to Jonson, we are deeply indebted.

Though it was certainly not so popular in its own time as the two types of comedy discussed above, in our day the comedy of manners has become the *sine qua non* of the Restoration theatre. Etherege, Wycherley, Congreve, Farquhar, and Vanbrugh are the five playwrights of this period who are most studied in college literature courses. These dramatists, though not the most representative of their age, are now acknowledged as the supreme arbiters of dramatic ingenuity and finesse.

Generally speaking, in their brilliant comedies, particularly of the first three playwrights mentioned, they presented what was then considered to be the best of all possible worlds. It was a most decorous society that was presented, ideally fashionable. John Palmer, in his *The Comedy of Manners* (1913), wrote what is still the most sensible and valuable statement on the world of these comedies: [20]

The comedies of Etherege are the natural product of an age for which life was an accepted pageant, incuriously observed, uncritically accepted stuff for a finished epigram. ... There was form and there

[20] Following John Palmer the best-proportioned criticisms of Restoration comedy are by: Bonamy Dobrée, *Restoration Comedy 1660-1720* (Oxford, 1924); Joseph Wood Krutch, *Comedy and Conscience after the Restoration* (New York, 1924); Kathleen M. Lynch, *The Social Mode of Restoration Comedy* (New York, 1926); Henry Ten Eyck Perry, *The Comic Spirit in Restoration Drama* (New Haven, 1925). Of the more recent critics Thomas H. Fujimura in his *The Restoration Comedy of Wit* (Princeton, 1952) and Dale Underwood in *Etherege and the Seventeenth Century Comedy of Manners* (New Haven, 1957) offer the most exciting expositions. Nevertheless, in my opinion, Fujimura loses the historical perspective he denies earlier critics in putting too much emphasis on the philosophical content of these plays. Also Underwood's book, written in a rather pretentious style, undeniably overstates his case in analyzing this comedy against a background of "Christianity and Christian humanism, the 'heroic' tradition, the honest-man tradition, and the tradition of courtly love" on the one hand, and on the other, "Philosophic and moral libertinism, Machiavellian and Hobbesian concepts as to the nature of man, and Machiavellian ethic."

was bad form. The whole duty of man was to find the one, and to eschew the other.[21]

Two types of persons moved in this society, people of "true wit and perfect fashion", and people who merely "ape the smartness of the time".[22] Thus an ordered society of highly specialized codes is presented, codes which embrace standards of speech, dress, interests, and ideals, and the one word that governed this eclectic code was "style". Comedy arises out of the contrast between those who adhere intelligently to the code, that is with style, and those who appear ridiculous through failing to do so. The latter group consists of those who attempt to conform too slavishly, and so overdo it, and those who either ignore it through disinterest or wilfully deviate.

The Man of Mode by Etherege was the earliest important comedy of manners, presented with enormous success in March, 1676. The hero, Dorimant, is often considered the perfect Restoration gentleman. Polished of manner, witty of tongue, and notably handsome, he also possesses the superb self-confidence that is necessary for success in amourous intrigue. And he is successful. By the end of the first act the audience learns that Dorimant has already seduced one lady, is about to seduce another, is planning for the seduction of still another, has ultimate designs on a friend's wife, and is blamed as being the "ruin" of a fallen woman. His sexual appetite alone, and the variety it seeks, would warrant admiration. Belinda may believe that Dorimant is "a man of no principles", but in the light of Restoration doctrine, she is wrong. The principle was to be clever and successful in the securing of one's satisfactions, and to this principle he is true. His inconstancy is of no matter. Nor is his heartlessness, that which has reaped for him so much condemnation from later critics of the drama. He succeeds where he seeks, and he succeeds with style.

Dorimant's ludicrous opposite is Sir Fopling Flutter, the "false" man of mode. His devotion to his appearance and to his social engagements is without any sense of proportion. His fatuous courting of Loveit naturally ends in a fiasco. Yet he is too witless even

[21]   John Leslie Palmer, *The Comedy of Manners* (London, 1913), p. 91.
[22]   Page 86.

to recognize the significance of a woman's rebuff. When Loveit calls him a fool at the close of the play, he contentedly claims that "an intrigue now would be but a temptation to me to throw away that vigour on one which I mean shall shortly make my court to the whole sex in a ballet". Sir Fopling wants to be essentially what Dorimant is; unfortunately, without any sense of decorum and degree, he becomes merely a hideous excuse for his ideal. Still, to the spectator, whether in the seventeenth century or today, his deviations are immensely comic.

Such contrasts are to be found among the ladies as well. In Congreve's *The Way of the World* the fat and fiftiesh Lady Wishfort's frenetic attempts to ensnare a man heighten, in delightfully comic contrast, the ideal woman as pictured in her niece Millamant. Hiding her womanly emotions behind a mask of cool gaiety, Millamant knows what she wants and she aims to get it. Note her famed "proviso" scene with Mirabell, the ideal in feminine behavior. Of especial interest is her management of Mirabell. For she is on an intellectual and moral level with her man, a position, according to George Meredith, that women must have in lofty comedy. Millamant's social and intellectual finesse in these scenes would almost convince one of Meredith's theory.

Though it is still conceded by most historians of English drama that the influence of Molière was marked in these dazzling dramas of wit, the native English origins are more closely regarded. Certainly the wit combats were not a new invention. Talk for talk's sake has had a noble tradition in English comedy. Shakespeare abounds with it. Even earlier the sophisticated repartee in the airy comedies of Lyly found much favor at the court of Queen Elizabeth. Likewise the subject matter of Restoration comedy was prevalent enough in native drama. In Shakespeare, marriage may have been considered an idealized state for lovers, but long before the Interregnum sex-antagonism was to be noticed in the theatre. A dislike for marriage and a desire for sexual freedom are suggested in the plays of Marston, Middleton, Brome, and Shirley. In addition, the cynical rakes and witty widows, such stereotypes later, were evident in Fletcher's works.

Topmost of all in influence on the comedy of manners was Ben

Jonson. Nor was it alone for his wits and would-bes which were transferred to Restoration drama, James Shirley being the chief intermediary. The basic spirit of Jonson's plays had its effect, for they too were realistic portrayals of contemporary manners. Only the society differs. His society was of the low life, whereas the Restoration dramatists portrayed high life. His wit battles were the abusive harangues of braggarts and bullies, not the arch witticisms of fops and belles. And in his gross caricature he hammered heavily his satirical blows. Moreover, social standards determined that the satire of the Restoration be of quite a different texture. Notwithstanding these differences, often stark in appearance, one must not forget this basic relationship between these two comedies, for here the Comic Spirit is strongly allied.

Perhaps in no other playwright of this turbulent century can be found more shadings and blendings of these three types of comedy than in the works of Sir William Davenant. His career spanning the years from James I to Charles II, he witnessed and was influenced by the whimsical tastes of theatre audiences. Being a man who had no desire to be unnoticed, he would certainly not ignore what the public wanted. Not always did his ability equal his aim, however, and he would sometimes fail, but generally his shrewd showmanship primed him as to what his audiences would find amusing. As a result he seldom tried to lead them in laughter. Rather he followed their leads, and thus he is a fine barometer of how tastes and fashions in theatrical comedy can change within the span of one man's career.

III

DAVENANT'S COMEDIES

In the following three chapters I shall study Davenant's dramaturgic treatment of the Comic Spirit in its relationship to the other
drama of the time and to the life of that age.[1] In this chapter I
shall discuss his only two full length original comedies, *The Wits*
and *News from Plymouth,* as well as two scenes of his Restoration
piece, *A Playhouse to be Let.* Chapter IV will deal with his tragicomedies and the means used to integrate the comic with the tragic.
Chapter V will be concerned with his adaptations and translations
of other comedies, namely those of Shakespeare, for which he has
been unjustly maligned. This analysis, following a brief account of
the play's history and a necessary plot summary, will depend
mainly on the plot and characterization, with occasional emphasis
on the importance of setting. Wholly dependent on these is the
Comic Spirit. By this means we can evaluate with more justice
Davenant's rightful position in the history of seventeenth-century
English comedy.

[1] The collection of Davenant's plays used for this study was *The Dra-
matic Works of Sir William D'Avenant, with prefatory Memoir and Notes,*
edd. J. Maidment and W. H. Logan, 5 vols. (Edinburgh-London, 1872-74).
Recently, in 1964, this same edition was reprinted in five volumes by
Russell and Russell, Inc. The printing has been limited to four hundred sets.
   In addition the comedies and tragicomedies included in the following
collections were read: *The Works of Beaumont and Fletcher,* ed. A. R.
Waller, 10 vols. (Cambridge, 1905-12); *The Dramatic Works of Richard
Brome,* 3 vols. (London, 1873); *The Works of Congreve,* ed. F. W. Bateson
(London, 1930); *The Dramatic Works of Thomas Dekker,* ed. Fredson
Bowers, 3 vols. (Cambridge, 1953-58); *The Dramatic Works of Sir George
Etherege,* ed. H. F. B. Brett-Smith, 2 vols. (Oxford, 1925); *The Complete
Works of George Farquhar,* ed. Charles Stonehilly, 2 vols. (Bloomsbury,

THE WITS

Destined to be his most successful comedy, *The Wits* almost never had a theatrical production. Sir Henry Herbert, His Majesty's master of the revels, and a somewhat sanctimonious custodian of public morals, refused to grant it a license. Through the timely intervention of Endymion Porter, Davenant's sponsor at court, the dispute was brought before the King. After due delay, Charles summoned Herbert to discuss the objections concerned, and swiftly each was settled. To realize how captious Herbert could be, one must take note of the following entry in his own journal:

This morning being the 9th of January, 1633, the Kinge was pleasd to call mee into his withdrawinge chamber to the windowe, wher he went over all that I had croste in Davenants play-booke, and allowing of *faith* and *slight* to bee asseverations only, and no oathes, markt them to stande, and some other few things, but in the greater part allowed of my reformations. This was done upon a complaint of Mr. Endymion Porters in December. The kinge is pleasd to take *faith, death, slight,* for asseverations, and no oaths to which I doe humbly submit as my masters judgment; but under favour, conceive them to be oaths, and enter them here, to declare my opinion and submission.[2]

Licensed on January 19, 1634, *The Wits* was acted first at the Blackfriars, where its reception was negative. A few days later a private performance at Court was accorded enthusiasm. When the theatres reopened in the Restoration, it was one of the first plays to be produced, was soon favored with repeated visits of that inveterate theatre-goer Samuel Pepys, and thereafter continued to

---

1930); *The Plays and Poems of Henry Glapthorne*, 2 vols. (London, 1874); *The Complete Plays of Ben Jonson*, Introduction by Felix E. Schelling, 2 vols. (London, 1925-35); *The Works of John Marston*, ed. A. H. Bullen, 3 vols. (London, 1887); *The Works of Thomas Middleton*, ed. A. H. Bullen, 8 vols. (Boston, 1885-86); *The Dramatic Works and Poems of James Shirley*, ed. William Gifford, 6 vols. (London, 1833); *The Complete Works of Sir John Vanbrugh*, ed. Bonamy Dobrée, 4 vols. (Bloomsbury, 1927-28); *The Complete Works of William Wycherley*, ed. Montague Summers, 4 vols. (Soho, 1924).
[2] Sir Henry Herbert, *The Dramatic Records of Sir Henry Herbert, Master of the Revels, 1623-1673*, ed. Joseph Quincy Adams (New Haven, 1927), p. 22.

enjoy a rousing audience response on into the eighteenth century.

The plot, with its farcical twists, is sharply organized to enhance the ludicrous antics of two would-be wits. Elder Pallatine and Sir Morglay Thwack, two country gentlemen, upon reaching those middle years so often dangerous to the masculine ego, to say nothing of the libido, arrive in London to satisfy both by means of their wits. That is, through mental ingenuity they plan to enjoy the life of town gallants at no financial expense to themselves. Endowed only with fine clothes, a few crowns of money, and much "wit and good counsel", they expect not only to woo fair ladies but also to fleece them of their wealth. Their one mutual agreement, and one fated to founder, is that Elder Pallatine will have all the female youth of the town, whereas Thwack must comfort himself with those ladies aged from forty to eighty years.

Neither seems aware that to use one's wits wisely in the town, one must know the ways of the town. And this they do not know. But there are those who do, namely Young Pallatine, a younger brother who is understandably vexed when denied financial aid from his smugly satisfied brother. Nevertheless, when counselled condescendingly to live by his wits, he proposes to do so. Assisted by Meager and Pert, two friends recently returned from the wars, and incited by the chiding remarks of the exasperated Lucy whom he loves, he propels his plan with uncommon sureness. Lady Ample, the prime target of the aging Lotharios, readily assents to his suggestions. At her first interview she adroitly manipulates the gentlemen to explain their "London business" and even feigns interest in the Elder Pallatine. Both men are instantly duped.

Meanwhile, Younger Pallatine's machinations become more imaginative. Elder Pallatine is informed that a mysterious lady of fortune, possessed with an unbounded passion for his person, seeks his company. Promising to follow their directions to cure her of her malady by solemn doctrine, resorting to the fleshly pleasures only as a last resort, he is led to a dingy dwelling, obviously long decrepit. The sordidness of these surroundings is explained away by the lady's desire for anonymity. It is a time-worn trick that any city man might have suspected. As soon as his clothes are removed, whatever is of value is appropriated surreptitiously by

Younger Pallatine, who leaves just before the constable arrives to arrest a destitute bawd. Naturally, Elder Pallatine becomes accused. However, wealth, the only sort of "wit" that proves effective for Elder Pallatine in this scene, manages to outwit Snore, the constable, when the latter is bribed with a ring. Thus Elder Pallatine is released to find Thwack, whom he in turn attracts to the lair with an enticing tale about a Mogul's daughter. After Thwack is ushered into the custody of the law as the supposed he-bawd, Elder Pallatine resumes his pursuit of Lady Ample.

This ingenious lady is waiting for him on her couch, supposedly dying. Her expressed wish is to will him her fortune, but in return she asks only that he accompany her in death. Astonished by her irrational request, though avid for the inheritance, he uncomfortably prevaricates. Meanwhile, matters are complicated by a subplot when Sir Tyrant Thrift, the lady's miserly guardian, is announced. Against his inclinations, Elder Pallatine is hurriedly hidden in a closed chest, and here he remains almost suffocated until after Thrift's departure, when a wicket at one end of the chest is opened to reveal to the hard-pressed suitor a very vigorous Lady Ample and a jubilant younger brother. The scene concludes with his muffled screams as his "coffin" is removed for burial.

The concluding scenes, rich in action, move with haste. Thwack is released through the assistance of Younger Pallatine and instantly engages himself in another venture, this time to steal the burial casket of Lady Ample, which is reputed to contain her jewels. Thrift, as well, is eager for the spoils, and it is he who is apprehended as a grave-robber. By this time both country "bumpkins" are wise to their folly and ready for repentance. Thwack's conversion assures Younger Pallatine as his heir. Elder Pallatine, severely chastened, eventually wins the Lady Ample, but not before he must accede to her request without question, a request that will assure Younger Pallatine's future. In addition, the moneybags of the vanquished Thrift are added to the rising prospects of the young victors. At the conclusion, true wits having been witnessed, the principals leave to attend the marriage of the Younger Pallatine to an enraptured Lucy.

The central plot concerning two aged country fools being duped by more sophisticated city-dwellers is certainly not original with Davenant. Middleton's play *Michaelmas Term* (1604-6) has a theme of a gulled country man. Then, too, in an earlier drama of Middleton's, *Blurt, Master Constable* (1602), Curvetto, an old courtier, is subjected to several practical jokes during his eager pursuit of amorous adventure. One of these occurs when he is mistaken for a thief while climbing a ladder into the house of the supposedly waiting Imperia, a trick that is closely reminiscent of the Mogul's niece incident. Moreover, in the same Middleton play a like fate awaits a Spaniard, Lazarello de Tormes. It is not improbable that these two gentlemen suggested the later Thwack and Elder Pallatine, even though they possess more exaggerated peculiarities than do their successors. Still another Middleton play may be an influence. Elder Pallatine, following his discovery that he has been outwitted, has a speech that is most like another speech in *The Widow*. In *The Wits*, Elder Pallatine, after being seized by Snore, says: [3]

I like this plot; the Lady Ample and my brother have most rare triumphant wits. Now by this hand I am most eagerly in love with both. I find I have deserv'd all and resolv'd to hug them and their designs though they affect me more and more, whither must I go? (Vol. II, p. 215)

In *The Widow*, Riccardo, a young gallant, says when he is arrested by officers for the "widow's business":

I thank her heartily, sh'as taught me wit; for had I been any but an ass, I should ha' begun with her indeed. By this light, the widow's a not able housewife! She bestirs herself. I have a greater mind to her now than e'er I had: I cannot go to prison for one I love better, I protest; that's one comfort. (Act II, Scene ii)

Beaumont and Fletcher also dealt with similar themes. In *Wit Without Money* (1614) by Beaumont there is an eccentric spendthrift named Valentine who despises wealth, and who believes that man should live by his wits alone. He, too, has a similar attitude to his younger brother Francisco. When the latter asks for

---

[3] Henceforth all references to Davenant's plays will provide volume number and page number. In contrast all quotations from plays by other authors will provide only the Act and Scene numbers.

one hundred pounds, Valentine's retort is that he must use his wits. However, here the similarities end, for Valentine is a misogynist, and Francisco has no inclination to humble his elder brother. A more valuable similarity would be seen in Beaumont's *Wit at Several Weapons* where Sir Perfidious Oldcraft boasts to his son that "Thou knowst all that I have, I ha' got by my wits" (I), as he tries to impress upon Witty-pate that he will help him only when the youth proves he can live by his wits. The second act of this play supports the relationship more fully when we note that Witty-pate is planning to gull his own father.

The problems involved when only one holds the purse strings with others dependent upon them are always timely, but especially so in the seventeenth century when young gentlemen were frequently at the none-too-tender mercies and whims of their fathers and elder brothers. Thus, when we note in Vanbrugh's Restoration play *The Relapse* that Young Fashion must make a fool out of his selfish elder brother, Lord Foppington, before he can make his own penurious plight noticed, it would be too strained an inference to think that Vanbrugh was influenced by either Davenant or Beaumont. Rather, he merely helped himself to a theme that was common to the social fabric and, thereby, always of general interest.

Other aspects of this Davenant plot are enough akin to other dramas to be worthy of mention. The hilarious episode in which Lady Ample fakes a fatal illness in order to spur the ridiculous greed of Elder Pallatine belongs to the stock situation of a lover counterfeiting some physical ailment in order to get sympathy. Such is true in several plays of the Beaumont and Fletcher canon. In *The Scornful Lady* Loveless feigns death for such a purpose. Better still is *The Wild Goose Chase* wherein Oriana pretends madness for love in order to win affection of one Mirabel. Years later in the Restoration, Etherege's *The Comical Revenge: or, Love in a Tub* has the following stage direction:

Sir Frederick is brought in upon a Bier, with a mourning Cloth over him, attended by a Gentleman in a mourning Cloak: Four Fillers carry the Corps, with their Instruments tuck'd under their Cloaks. (IV, vii)

The reason for such solemn panoply is that Sir Frederick may

enlist the attentions and sympathy of the Widow he has been heretofore courting in vain. Closer perhaps to the reasons for such pre-
tence in *The Wits* is the justly famous *Volpone*. In this dark comedy Jonson has his horrifying hero feign a fatal illness in order to
win from avaricious would-be heirs rich and handsome gifts. Lady
Ample's plan is almost the same, though fortunately her attitude
in determining such action, unlike that of Volpone, remains in the
comic realm.

Blurt, Master Constable can again be identified with this play.
In the Middleton drama the business about Blurt the constable
and his cronies corresponds in idea to that of Snore in this play. It
is a tenuous relationship, to be sure, though something more than
coincidence may be present in that Blurt repeatedly refers to the
Duke for whom he acts just as Snore speaks continually in the
name of the king.

To a Shakespearean this low comedy episode may faintly recall
the Dogberry scenes in *Much Ado About Nothing*.[4] Nothing in
the dialogue is directly borrowed, but in spirit there seems to be
harmony. Particularly is this true of the revised version of the
play, altered in the Restoration to suit a changing audience. Although Davenant has still avoided an accusation of outright
plagiarism, the scene wherein Snore is examining the eight Watch-
men, these men being additions in the revised version, and the
corresponding scene when Dogberry and Verges examine the
prisoners, are almost identical in atmosphere. Here, too, one
recognizes that Davenant was aware of his Shakespeare when
elaborating his characterization of Snore, for where he was formerly a mere ass, he has become a pompous ass. The new Snore and
Dogberry would be close competitors in a contest to judge the
quintessence of official foolery.

No one other person in Davenant's drama can be so closely
identified with another playwright's character, with the possible
exceptions of Thwack and the play's hero. Sir Morglay Thwack
in his designs on women resembles Falstaff in *The Merry Wives*

---

[4]   A good study of low comedy is Ola Elizabeth Winslow, *Low Comedy as
a Structural Element in English Drama from the beginnings to 1642*
(Menasha, Wis., 1926).

of Windsor, a play we are reminded of again when Elder Pallatine is hid in a chest to avoid being seen by Lady Ample's guardian, a scene that is not unlike Falstaff's hiding in a clothes basket in order to avoid being detected by a husband. Young Pallatine, the clever and riotous young gallant, eager for pleasure, is representative of a common type that requires only a little more spit and polish to become the hero of a Restoration comedy of manners. If one were to demand an influence, another play by Middleton might be cited. In *A Mad World, My Masters* the personality of Dick Follywit is very much akin to our hero. His comrades, as well, Penitent Brothel, Lieutenant Mawword, and Ancient Hoboy, correspond to Pert and Meager. And since Dick's grandfather, Sir Bounteous Progress, refuses to give him any money, he resolves to gull the old man. Nevertheless, no more than this is similar. Sir Bounteous Progress, being quite a different man from Elder Pallatine, his personality demands quite different methods if he is to be effectively gulled. Nevertheless, like several other characters in this drama, Young Pallatine has his likenesses elsewhere because he has been deliberately created as a recognized type in order to gain quickly audience understanding, but beyond that no direct influence is determinable.

The kind of comedy provided by this plot and characterization is heavily indebted to the success of Ben Jonson. In *Epicoene* (1608) Jonson portrays a sustained contrast ot the true wits with the false wits, laughter arising from the spontaneous suavity of the one and the pretentious crudity of the other. This was a distinction that was to be of great influence on the Restoration comedy of manners. But immediately it was not so significant, though it was in time imitated by the lesser dramatists. For plotting Davenant appropriated this social philosophy, and in characterization he relied heavily on Jonson's humors as well. Still, he made both his own.

The basic plot of two would-be wits being duped by true wits lends itself to a great deal of comic irony. Elder Pallatine and Thwack think that they are clever; we know they are not. They suppose they are trapping Lady Ample, whereas all the time that wily lady is playing them for country clowns. It is such irony as this that usually generates the sort of Hobbesian laughter wherein we would feel somewhat superior to these two men. But not quite! They can quarrel like two spoiled boys, and they do this frequently, yet Davenant in characterizing them never makes them as stupid as Jonson would have been inclined. Nor do they even forfeit our sympathy as such types often do in Jonson's comedies. Both men are not dullards; rather they are merely naive, allowing their over-estimation of their not inconsiderable abilities to trip them into temporary disgrace. Thwack, to his credit, never blames anyone but himself for his foolishness, and at the end he is much too goodhearted to feel malice towards another for injuries received. As for Elder Pallatine, he eventually recognizes the justice of his cure, and thus we do not begrudge his final triumph in winning Lady Ample.

Because Davenant is fond of his two gulls, the laughter we give is not condescending. Rather, because he makes us like them our mirth comes from a recognition that we, too, can often overestimate our potential. Thus in all their farcical episodes, we laugh freely. And because this plot abounds with farce, even boisterous horseplay at times, our laughter is unrestrained. In contrast to them, though, is Sir Tyrant Thrift, a genuine Jonsonian humor. His obsession is money, an obsession he could never conceal with success. During his interview with his apparently dying niece, his greed is so gross that he veers close to being a dark character. Cleverly Davenant introduces him in this scene immediately after Elder Pallatine's vain efforts at legacy-hunting in order to divide dramatically his characters, making it clear that Elder Pallatine's motives, unlike Thrift's, are more absurd than reprehensible. Thrift makes us laugh, it is true, but never comfortably so. Therefore we are pleased with his downfall at the play's denouement.

Streaked throughout this play is a vein of comedy that was to blaze brightly in the eighteenth century. The love element of Young Pallatine and Lucy smacks of sentimental comedy, a genre yet undeveloped. In the first act we see Lucy's sorrow in loving a gay spendthrift. But since Davenant has suggested clearly that Young Pallatine's weaknesses are merely youthful peccadilloes and not the result of a twisted mind, we smile at both her fears

and her tears. We never really laugh. Such a saccharine sweet reaction as this does not result from vibrant comedy, but it was
pleasant enough theatrical fare to make it highly desirable almost
a century later in such plays as Richard Cumberland's *The West
Indian*.

So far we have noticed that *The Wits* as comedy adheres to its
period. Only through Lady Ample do we see a marked anticipation of a comedy to come, the Restoration comedy of manners.
This cool lady could well hold her own with Millamant and her
Restoration sisters. Reared by a stingy guardian, she is obliged to
supplement his niggardly allowance by the use of her wits. No
wonder she is disdainful of the male species. When she hears that
Lucy had been hoodwinked by Young Pallatine, she has a biting
reproach for the girl's "apostacy in wit".

> Thy feature and thy wit are wealth enough
> To keep thee high in all those vanities
> That wild ambition, or expensive pride,
> Perform in youth; but thou invest'st their use:
> Thy lover, like the foolish adamant,
> The steel, thou fiercely doest allure, and draw
> To spend thy virtue, not to get by it. (II, 140)

Thus she commands the weeping girl to redeem the credit of her
sex by deliberate device. Hardly is this accomplished when her
aging country suitors arrive to be unwarily subjected to her sarcastic taunts, addressed mainly to their rustic backgrounds, a
theme frequently expounded in the later comedy of manners.[5]
Aided by Lucy, who has obviously learned her lesson well, she
decries country life with a tartness that betters similar sentiments
expressed by Harriet in the fifth act of Etherege's *The Man of
Mode:*

Amp: Stay, gentlemen, Good souls! they have seen, Lucy,
      The country turtle's bill, and think our lips,
      I' th' town and court, are worn for the same use.
Lucy: Pray how do the ladies there? poor villagers,

---

[5] It is interesting to note that Shirley's *The Lady of Pleasure*, licensed in
1635, has a character, Lady Bornwell, who rails against country life in a
similar fashion. I. i.

They churn still, keep their dairies, and lay up
For embroidered mantles against the heir's birth.

Amp: Who is begot i' th' Christmas holidays.

E.P.: Yes, surely, when the spirit of
Mince-pie reigns in the blood.

Amp: What? penny gleek I hope's
In fashion yet, and the treacherous foot
Not wanting on the table frame, to jog
The husband, lest he lose the noble, that
Should pay the grocer's man for spice and fruit.

Lucy: The good old butler shares too with his lady
In the box, bating for candles that were burnt
After the clock struck ten.

Thw: He doth indeed.
Poor country madams, th'are in subjection still
The beasts, their husbands, make 'em sit on three
Legg'd stools, like homely daughters of an hospital,
To knot socks for their cloven feet.

E.P.: And when these tyrant husbands, too, grow old,
As they have still th' impudence to live long,
Good ladies, they are fain to waste the sweet
And pleasant seasons of the day in boiling
Jellies for them, and rolling little pills
Of cambric lint to stuff their hollow teeth.

Lucy: And then the evenings, warrant ye, they
Spend with Mother Spectacle, the curate's wife,
Who does inveigh 'gainst curling and dyed cheeks;
Heaves her devout impatient nose at oil
Of jessamine, and thinks powder of Paris more
Prophane than th' ashes of a Romish martyr.

Amp: And in the days of joy and triumph, sir,
Which come as seldom to them as new gowns,
Then, humble wretches! they do frisk and dance
In narrow parlours to a single fiddle,
That squeaks forth tunes like a departing pig.

Lucy: Whilst the mad hinds shake from their feet more dirt
Than did the cedar roots, that danc'd to Orpheus.

Amp: Do they not pour their wine too from an
Ewer, or small gilt cruce, like orange-water kept
To sprinkle holiday beards?

Lucy: And when a stranger comes, send seven
Miles post by moon-shine for another pint! (II, 146-147)

Lady Ample represents the Restoration ideal of a woman being equal to man in all respects. She is without sentimentality, she is eminently practical, and she is still beautiful, intelligent, and incisively witty. In fact, she goes one step farther than many Restoration heroines. Her wit triumphs over man's. Before consenting to marry, she, like the Wife of Bath's heroine, demands her suitor's unconditional surrender. Entirely subdued, Elder Pallatine good-naturedly admits her "better wit" and power to reduce him to "quietness, meek sufferings, and patient awe". Lady Ample is not man's equal; she is his superior.

Notwithstanding the variety of virtues mentioned here, still *The Wits* would be no better than many another comedy of its time were it not for the realism of its setting, London. Some of this realism is imparted through what is spoken and how it is spoken. Already we have discussed the central characters enough to suggest that though they are not profound characterizations, they are bold ones. There is no blurring of characters here; each is distinct from the other. Lucy, skilled as she is at repartee, would never be mistaken for Lady Ample, for Lucy is too feminine, too yielding and sentimental. Nor would Sir Morglay Thwack be confused with Elder Pallatine even if both do succumb to the same tricks. Thwack is a sort of music hall joker, given to coarse jests and sudden pratfalls, whereas his cohort feigns a veneer of sophistication. It is such people as these who display the variety of a cosmopolitan centre.

Even in the Snore episodes there is little likelihood that Mistress Snore, the constable's wife, could be mistaken for Mistress Queasy, her neighbor. Mistress Queasy's sole interest is her rent, and convinced that her tenant, a known bawd, has absconded without paying it, she is adamant that the constable pursue the felon, no matter how late the hour. Mistress Snore, however, has more to lament. She is a woman, highly sexed, but little satisfied. Not being promiscuous she vents her frustrations in accusing her insensitive husband of infidelities, venting a volley of abuse at her neighbor, or eagerly eyeing a man she thinks is involved in prostitution. For such a woman it must be a trial to have a husband who spends his nights searching for bawds and whores. It is not surprising that she says "a woman had / As good marry a colestaff as a constable." With only a slight change in the play's tone such a character could be a tragic victim of circumstances. But here she is safely kept on a comic level. Fortunately for us she is so excitable, for her tense emotions stimulate a fishwifely exchange of words that provides much local color:

Que: Good mistress Snore, forbear your husband but
        To-night and let the search go on.
M.Sn: I will not forbear; you might ha' let your house
        To honest women, not to bawds. Fie upon you!
Que: Fie upon me! 'tis well known I'm the mother
        Of children! scurvy fleak! 'tis not for naught
        You boil eggs in your gruel: and your man Sampson
        Owes my son-in-law, the surgeon, ten groats
        For turpentine, which you have promis'd to pay
        Out of his Christmas box.
M.Sn: I defy thee.
        Remember thy first calling; thou set'st up
        With a peck of damsons and a new sieve;
        When thou brok'st at Dowgate corner, 'cause the boys
        Flung down thy ware.
Sn: Keep the peace, wife; keep the peace!
M.Sn: I will not peace: she took my silver thimble
        To pawn when I was a maid; I paid her
        A penny a month use.
Que: A maid! yes, sure;
        By that token, goody Tongue, the midwife,
        Had a dozen napkins o' your mother's best
        Diaper, to keep silence, when she said
        She left you at Saint Peter's fair, where you
        Long'd for pig.   (II, 163-164)

A few lines later Elder Pallatine, bewildered at being mistaken for a he-bawd, explains, "Good faith, you may as soon / take me for a whale, which is something rare, / You know, o'this side the bridge." To this Mistress Snore exclaims:

               This indeed:
    Yet our Paul was in the belly of one,
    In my Lord Mayor's show; and, husband, you remember
    He beckoned you out of the fish's mouth,
    And you gave him a pippin, for the poor soul
    Had like to have choak'd for very thirst. (II, 166)

This sort of dialogue does not advance the plot at all, but it does provide the local color which makes the plot seem possible. Events take on a reality they would not have otherwise. Jonson knew the value of such realistic touches, and Davenant has evidently discerned it.

Other injections of local color continually appear. The play opens with a discussion of warfare. Pert and Meager, having just returned from bearing arms, are in no mood to glamorize their recent enterprise, no more than the soldiers depicted in many an earlier play. Pert, with caustic irony, says to Young Pallatine,

> Faith!
> We have been to kill, we know not whom,
> Nor why: led on to break a commandment
> With the consent of custom and the laws. (II, 121)

Meager's mission appears to have been more for adventure:

> Mine was a certain inclination, sir,
> To do mischief where good men of the jury,
> And a dull congregation of grey-beards
> Might urge no tedious statute 'gainst my life.

Obviously these two weary soldiers have considered their armed service with some doubt, and we may well infer that it was a doubt common to the soldiers of that age. With a king requiring an army soon, it is well that Davenant put into the mouth of Young Pallatine the only possible explanation:

> Nothing but honour could seduce thee, Pert!
> Honour! which is the hope of the youthful
> And the old soldier's wealth, a jealousy
> To the noble, and myst'ry to the wise.

The vogue for bogus spiritual tracts with their quaint alliterative titles is briefly the subject of satire:

Pert: And can you mollify the mother, sir,
      In a strong fit?
E.P.: Sure, gentlemen, I can,
      If books penn'd with a clean and wholesome spirit
      Have any might to edify. Would they
      Were here!

Meag: What, sir?
E.P.: A small library,
     Which I was wont to make companion to
     My idle hours; where some, I take it, are
     A little consonant unto this theme.
Pert: Have they not names?
E.P.: A pill to purge phlebotomy, – A balsamum
     For the spiritual back. – A lozenge against lust;
     With divers others, sir, which, though not penn'd
     By dull platonic Greeks, or Memphian priests,
     Yet have the blessed mark of separation
     Of authors silenc'd, for wearing short hair. (II, 159)

Plainly this passage was so well received that in the folio edition
the last speech is altered in this manner:

E.P.: A pill to purge the pride of pagan patches,
     A lozenge for the lust of loytring love,
     And balsoms for the bites of Babel's beast:
     With many ...   (II, 159, footnote)

This realism of local color also extends to contemporary gossip.
Nor is the author squeamish when such chat obviously alludes to
his own disfigurement and its attributed cause. In one instance
when Lucy is vexed, she addresses her lover thus:

     Pall, you are as good-natur'd to me, Pall,
     As the wife of a silenc'd minister
     Is to a monarchy or to lewd gallants,
     That have lost a nose.   (II, 171)

Thick-skinned Davenant could take a jest directed at himself,
particularly if it meant his play would have one more boisterous
laugh.

     The success of this realism hinges mainly on Davenant's skill
in dialogue. Charles I noticed this, for Herbert reports that he
"commended the language, but dislikt the plott and characters".[6]
Several decades later Pepys wrote kindly of the similes which he
thought "mighty good".[7] To be sure, Davenant did have a decided

---

[6]   Herbert, p. 54.
[7]   Pepys' diary entry for January 18, 1669.

knack in writing lively speeches, brisk in thought and imaginative in conception. One of his favorite devices was the use of metaphors and similes. At times he emphasized the diminutive, to be noted when he derides Meager's meagre possessions:

> do not I know,
> That a mouse yok'd to a peascod may draw
> With the frail cordage of one hair, your goods
> About the world. (II, 122)

It may be in the form of a maxim, as when Elder Pallatine smugly asserts the sense of his courting procedure:

> Disdain is like to water pour'd on ice
> Quenches the flame awhile to raise it higher. (II, 150)

And it can suggest aptly the humility of one's position. Elder Pallatine, in following his high hopes, is suddenly reduced to unflattering self-recognition when accused as a bawd:

> Confin'd in wainscot walls too,
> Like a liquorish rat, for nibbling
> Unlawfully upon forbidden cheese. (II, 167)

The rightness of these figures of speech is that they so well suit the situation, never existing for their own sake, but rather for expanding the value of that which they wish to explain. Although it is a common simile, to be sure, still it suits both the situation and the speaker when Pert describes Elder Pallatine preparing for his mysterious assignation:

> *E.P.:* Is he in bed?
> *Pert:* Not yet!
> But stripping in more haste than an old snake
> That hopes for a new skin. (II, 160)

The aptness of speech in illustrating character is best seen in the conception of Thwack. Like Dogberry, previously likened to Snore, he is given to humorous malapropisms, which heighten with wonderful humor his young ideas. When he is promised a Mogul's niece, he urges Elder Pallatine thus:

> Quick rogue! I cannot hold. Little thought I
> The Thwacks of the north should inoculate
> With the Moguls of the south.   (II, 177)

Thwack can be crude, unthinkingly so before ladies, but still such crudity suits his rustic frankness. This is so especially when he is at the mercy of a tactless female:

Amp: Why all for widows, sir? can nothing that
      Is young affect your mouldy appetite?
Thw: No in sooth; damsels at your years are wont
      To talk too much over their marmalade;
      They can't fare well, but all the town must hear't.
      Their love's so full of praises, and so loud,
      A man may with less noise lie with a drum. (II, 149)

Blunt as this dialogue is, though necessary to represent character accurately, it is never offensive. Except to the most prudish, this dialogue would never seem anything else but vigorously graphic, for it is always representative of its speaker. It cannot be divorced from the character. This ability to reflect his character's world through dialogue Davenant learned from Jonson and Middleton. And he practises it with a sureness that suggests the strength of the better Restoration playwrights who, through speech, would reflect a more fashionably exalted society.

For his first original comedy Davenant did quite well in welding together the various branches of comedy. Realistic in setting and topical in idea, he presented a plot, essentially ironic, that exploited the farcical, and he larded it all with injections of sentimental comedy, satire, and wit. Because he had the talent to blend them all without blurring any one, he produced a play that Dodsley, the eighteenth-century collector, found suitable to reprint. Having such luck on his first undertaking, it would be with expected difficulty that Davenant could equal it a second time.

NEWS FROM PLYMOUTH

With his next original comedy Davenant took upon himself the burden of preparing it for a different audience. Instead of pandering to courtly tastes, this time he decided to please the plebeians. Undoubtedly the reason for this commercial venture was financial. The monetary rewards of productions at Court were risky, particularly for a minor playwright on whom no one really depended. Public playhouses were more responsible in paying their just debts. On August 1, 1635, *News from Plymouth* was licensed and soon afterwards presented at the Globe. As far as it is known, following this initial performance it was never acted again. The reason for its apparent failure is not easily discernible. One would like to believe that circumstances beyond the play's worth itself, such as a poor performance, were responsible. Since no reports on this subject are extant, such an excuse is not likely to be forthcoming. It would be wiser to look at the play, excellent though it often is, to see why it might not suit a summer audience which is more accustomed, as stated in its Prologue, to "dancing, and buckler fights, than art or wit".

News from Plymouth has no centrally-organized plot. Instead it is an olla-podrida of episodes concerning the eternal battle of the sexes, all arranged with more vitality than harmony. Davenant himself anticipated unfavorable criticism when he wrote:

> For when you but survey the narrow ways
> We walk in; you will find we could not raise
> From a few seamen, wind-bound in a port
> More various changes, business, or more sport. (IV, 108)

The mariners referred to here are Seawit, Topsail, and Cable, three Sea-captains, who are stranded between voyages, windbound that is, in the port at Plymouth. Their present condition is not pleasant. Almost empty of pocket, they find Plymouth beyond their means, unbelievably expensive according to the exaggerations of Cable:

> This town is dearer than Jerusalem
> After a year's siege; they would make us pay
> For day-light, if they knew how to measure
> The sun-beams by the yard. Nay sell the very
> Air too if they could serve it out in fine
> China-bottles. If you walk but three turns
> In the High-street, they will ask you money
> For wearing out the pebbles. (IV, 111-112)

Nor does the sailor's proverbial diversion seem too tempting:

> And wildly destitute of women. Here
> Are none but a few matrons of Biscay,
> That the Spaniards left here
> In Eighty-eight.

But to Seawit their prospects hold some hope. He has news of a wealthy and lovely lady who is residing nearby. Lady Loveright and her cousin Mrs. Joynture are paying guests of the resourceful Widow Carrack. All three women are to provide the amorous complexities of the ensuing intrigues.

For five acts these sea-captains pursue the ladies, while the ladies, in their own way, pursue them. Quarrels result and friends become enemies. But in the end all ends well. Seawit, who has proved himself superior to his cronies in the artful game of love, seems to make headway with the sportive Loveright, but when she decides to accept the long-suffering Studious Warwell, he acquiesces to the eager entreaties of Joynture. Cable, whose sole interest is sex, not marriage, is finally reduced to begging the hand of the suddenly irresolute Widow. Topsail, without luck at all, resigns himself to the hope of finding a wife after his next sea voyage, and until then "honour's [his] mistress".

Adding variety to the above events are farcical subplots concerning some truly peculiar characters. Sir Solemn Trifle, a foolish old knight, and the uncle of Loveright, is given to gossip, sometimes of a dangerously political sort, and this indiscretion almost leads him into some serious trouble with the law. Then there is Seawit's charge, Sir Furious Inland, whose given name denotes all too aptly his choleric temper. Bragging frequently of his physical prowess, he surprisingly lives up to his own estimates, thus providing some of the gustiest passages in the play. During much of this bluster, Captain Bumble, a Dutchman with an hilariously funny accent, is his now-willing, now-unwilling foil. Though these sub-characters are meant merely to provide incidental mirth, their antics often tend to take over and direct the play away from its central episodes.

Sources for *News from Plymouth* are of chief concern in relation to characterization, no plot. Of the medley of plots contained herein, only one is directly related to a previous play, and it is of value for characterization as well as plot. Although Sir Solemn Trifle has been on the stage since Act One, amusing the audience with his garrulity, it is not until Act Four that we learn of his secret passion. Assisted by his underlings, Dash, Scarecrow, Zeal, and Prattle, he is concerned with disseminating various and often astounding items of news, both foreign and domestic, much of it having ominous portent for mankind. Topsail, who has been admitted to this confidence, later blackmails the foolish old knight into leaving the city so that Loveright and others might be freed of his annoying loquacity.

Obviously, Jonson's *The Staple of News* has influenced this brief sub-plot. Early in Jonson's play, the spectator is introduced to a news office with all of its departments, much of it discussed in considerable detail. As stated above, Davenant uses this episode only incidentally, and in his play there is really no news office as such, it being rather Trifle's home where he meets with his news despatchers. Still, there are further similarities to convince one of the value of Jonson's play as a source.

Just as we meet this avocation of Trifle through a visit paid to him by Topsail, in *The Staple of News* we meet the News Office when it is visited by the young spendthrift Pennyboy. Here he is informed of its purpose when Fitton acknowledges:

>   And dish out newes,
>   Were't true, or false.
> *Pen:* Why, me thinkes Sir, if the honest common people
>   Will be abus'd, why should not they ha' their pleasure,
>   In the believing Lyes, are made for them;
>   As you i'the Office, making them yourselves?
> *Fit:*   O Sir! it is the printing we oppose
> *Cym:* We not forbid that any Newes, be made,
>   But that 't be printed; for when Newes is printed,
>   It leaves Sir to be Newes . . .   (I, v)

In Davenant's play nothing is mentioned about an aversion to printing the news, but as presented we assume that the reports are carried only by word of mouth. Then, too, similar information regarding the manufacturing of the news, as expressed above, is voiced by Trifle:

> They come for news; man's nature's greedy of it.
> We wise men forge it; and the credulous vulgar,
> Our instruments, disperse it ...   (IV, 167-168)

Jonson's news office does seem to have a greater fund for information. Fitton and Cymbol claim to get the news from the following places among others:

Barbers newes, Taylors Newes, Porters, and Watermens newes, Coranti and Gazetti, vacation newes, Terme newes, Christmas newes, newes o'faction, Reformed newes, Protestant newes, Pontificiall newes, Day-bookes, Characters, Precedents.   (I, v.)

Trifle's explanation is,

> I have studied hard,
> Dash,
> And from the general courants, gazettes,
> Public and private letters from all parts
> Of Christendom, though they speak contraries
> Weigh'd and reduc'd 'em to such certainties,
> That I dare warrant 'em authentical
> Under my hand, and seal.   (IV, 168)

Dash, Scarecrow, Zeal, and Prattle, the Intelligencers who fetch the news from Trifle and then disperse it, would correspond to the various gazeteers in the Jonson play, who, on the other hand, supply the news as well as manufacture it.

As to the news mentioned, it is interesting to note that in both plays the first news mentioned concerns the Pope. In Jonson's play it is reported that the King of Spain has been elected Pope, whereas in Davenant, the item is still more sensational:

> ... on my credit,
> Though I grieve to report it, Rome is taken
> By the ships of Amsterdam, and the Pope himself,
> To save his life, turn'd Brownist.   (IV, 170)

Davenant's news regarding the Emperor is also more surprising.

Jonson has the Emperor resign to be replaced by the King of Spain, whereas Davenant predicts the Prince of Orange will become the Emperor before his sudden death on the October 10th next. Nor is this news of the fanciful variety only. At times it is quite timely. Jonson refers to the Fifth Monarchy men, and Davenant mentions Cardinal Richelieu and the Huguenots, an altercation of some importance then occurring across the Channel. Notwithstanding the more startling elements in the news coming from Trifle's office, it must be admitted that Jonson provides a richer variety, embracing such topics as submarines, alchemy, and cannibals. Of course it is remembered that the news office is the background for the entire Jonson play, giving it its title. Certainly the title *News from Plymouth* owes part of its origin to the Trifle plot, but not all of it.

Another Jonson play is a valuable source, mainly for character traits. Sir Politic Would-be in *Volpone*, like Trifle, possesses a great fund of information, and he too has followers who supply him with news. Both knights are pompous, irritatingly talkative, and insufferably smug in their self-confident belief that they are worldly wise. Consequently, both are to suffer as butts of practical jokes.

Undoubtedly Davenant was also aware of a play by James Shirley called *The Example*, which was licensed by the master of the revels the year before, in 1634. In it appears one Sir Solitary Plot, who, like the characters of Jonson and Davenant, is a "humor". Then, too, his name, as with the others, is descriptive of his failing. And again, like both, he suspects a plot in every circumstance, and thus can be cured only as the result of indignities suffered in a practical joke. As with this characterization likeness, there is also a plot similarity. In the Shirley play, Jacinta, the heroine, arranges a plot to frighten her uncle, Sir Solitary Plot. After having suitors disguised in order to beguile her uncle, she then gives him the severe fright of having the impostors apprehended as traitors. In *News from Plymouth*, however, it is not Trifle's niece who tricks him, even though she certainly would not be averse to such betrayal. Still, his fear is also instilled with a threat of a treason charge. In spite of these resemblances, the handling of the plot suggests that Davenant used Jonson for his principal source.[8]

Since there is no record of *News from Plymouth* being produced in the Restoration, it is likely that the Jonson drama influenced the two Restoration plays that have episodes resembling the above. In Durfey's *Sir Barnaby Whigg: Or, No Wit Like a Woman's* (1681) the title figure is full of dire rumors regarding the future, prophesying such natural disasters as plagues, fires, and famines. Because this play also contains one Captain Porpuss, a blunt sea-captain, who speaks only in nautical terms, certainly akin to the three sea captains in *News from Plymouth*, it would be unwise to rule out the influence of Davenant's play entirely. Even if *News from Plymouth* were not produced in the Restoration, that does not mean that it had disappeared from theatre collections to which many playwrights would have access. Also if one were inclined to borrow, it would be less risky to borrow from a forgotten play. About three years earlier in Otway's *Friendship in Fashion,* Victoria mentions to Guile one Malagere who keeps an Office of Intelligence for all the scandal in the town. The difference here, however, is that Malagere, who spreads his notorious gossip among Coffee-house companions and whispers it to the Orange-women at the playhouse, is obviously involved in this nasty business for purposes of finance. He is an ugly extension of a figure who began merely as an object of ridicule. Neither Jonson or Davenant would wish to lay claim to such a reprobate.

Another "humor" of esteemed pedigree is the country knight Sir Furious Inland, whose name, of course, suggests his "disease of quarreling". To him it is incomprehensible that any quarrel, however trifling, should be settled without bloodshed. Nor does it matter if the dispute involves his best friend; it is better to fight a friend than not fight at all. This braggadocio belongs, one would hasten to say, to the "miles gloriosus" type. One recalls Falstaff and Pistoll and many others who are talented boasters, often more

---

[8] Davenant may also have been aware of a play by Beaumont titled *The Woman Hater.* This play contains a number of Intelligencers who are actually spies with the job of ferreting out traitors. Still, they are not the same sort of Intelligencers as appear in *The Staple of News* or *News from Plymouth.*

skilful at the art than this furious fellow. Jonson's Bobadill, perhaps even Kastril, the quarreling boy in *The Alchemist*, come to mind. Still, Sir Furious surpasses them all. Davenant has created his own figure by making him no empty braggart, by making him a battler who really battles. Just find him a cause to champion and the cause will be vindicated. He may be ludicrous in performance – more likely to be so than not – but he will never yield the field.

Pitted against Sir Furious Inland is one whom Davenant has not made nearly so much his own. Bumble, the Dutch sea-captain, serves both as a necessary foil for a braggart, and, in his own right, as the possessor of an atrocious accent. Certainly the presentation of a foreign accent in order to provoke a laugh was an old theatrical device, and one that was never to die. Audiences love, perhaps with Hobbesian glee, to laugh at the customs and speech of foreigners. Catering to this phenomenon, playwrights usually exaggerate the idiosyncrasies of such characters. Shakespeare saw the value of it in his history plays, such as *II Henry IV* and *Henry V*. In Dekker's *The Honest Whore, Part Two*, Bryan, an Irish footman, is provided with an accent for purposes of comedy. In Middleton's *Anything for a Quiet Life*, Margarita, a French bawd, uses a comical dialect. Years later in Etherege's *The Comical Revenge: or, Love in a Tub*, Dufoy, listed as "a saucy impertinent French-man, Servant to Sir Frederick", is one of the first of the Restoration servants to provide hilarity by means of a quaintly spoken English. As for *The Dutch Courtezan*, Franceschina speaks with a Dutch accent, although it is certainly not for a comic purpose. Franceschina is a "heavy", existing only for serious consideration. In Middleton and Rowley's *The Fair Quarrel*, a Dutch nurse briefly appears in Act Three, and here the use of accent is undoubtedly for comedy, since there is no other visible reason for its employment. The greatest likeness to Davenant's Bumble is the Dutch Skipper in Thomas Dekker's *The Shoemaker's Holiday*, a blunt fellow whose accent serves definitely a comic purpose. Undoubtedly a playwright would evaluate his English audience's attitude towards the Dutch, or towards any other foreigner, before deciding whether the accent could be used to suggest mirth or malevolence.

Related to the use of a foreign accent is the skill with which Davenant has his three captains use nautical language, often in metaphors and similes, to express their thoughts. Topsail is fond of these sea-going expressions to emphasize his pursuit of the female:

> Small hands, full breasts, soft lips, and sparkling eyes!
> If I can board her, she'll prove lawful prize. (IV, 123)

Such marine terminology was to be used again in the Restoration, thus depicting the comic incongruity of applying specialized language to an alien field. Captain Porpuss in Durfey's *Sir Barnaby Whigg* has already been mentioned. More justly famous, though, is Ben, the "half home-bred, half sea-bred" son of Sir Sampson in Congreve's *Love for Love*. As with Topsail, Cable, and Seawit, Ben's sexual drive is amazing, and like them he tempers its ferocity for our sensibilities by always considering it in expressions belonging to only the sailor's world.

Of these three sea-captains, surely Cable is the most interesting both to us and to his contemporaries for his bullish disinclination to marry. Still, he is not to have his way. As man veers from the social ethics, it is woman who intervenes to return him to it. The spectator is not surprised to see a humbled Cable in Act Five imploring a suddenly coy Carrack to marry him. His deviation from the norm has come full circle, providing much amusement in the process. Such a dislike of marriage was seen as an element in earlier comedy. Although Shakespeare never showed it particular favor, in Elizabethan drama it was a common motif. Mirabell in *The Wild Goose Chase* expresses his idea on the subject with unmistakeable brevity:

> but, for marriage,
> I neither yet believe in't, nor affect it;
> Nor think it fit. (I, iii)

However, such an attitude is much more common in Restoration comedy, exemplified later in Congreve's Mirabell. There is scarcely a comedy of this period in which there is not at least one character who has this view of the matrimonial yoke. Such is to be expected in a period when the relationships between the sexes was

seldom moral in the conventional sense, and almost never senti-
mentalized.[9]

In discussing *The Wits* we noted a couple of males who might
have been in Shakespeare's *The Merry Wives of Windsor*. In this
play it is a female, Widow Carrack, who reminds one of the merry
wives. Ingenious in contriving situations that will stimulate Cable's
amorous interest, she is stubborn in her determination to yield
only on her own terms. And like Shakespeare's Mrs. Ford and
Mrs. Page she is blithely insensitive to any indignities she may
visit upon her perplexed suitor. This boisterous woman is very
much the Elizabethan in spirit and flesh. On the other hand, Lady
Loveright prefigures the Restoration heroine. Unmistakably an
extension of Lady Ample in *The Wits*, this very independent
woman has definite ideas regarding the man she will marry. Her
explanation to Joynture as to why she has rebuffed the importuni-
ties of the wealthy Sir Studious Warwell reads thus:

Love: ... the great estate commended
     In this Sir Studious Warwell was a hindrance,
     And no way did advance my favours to him.
     I have enough, and my ambition is
     To make a man, not take addition from him.
     I would have him poor, and if unlearn'd the better;
     I cannot feed on the philosopher's banquet,
     Nor would I have my bed-fellow a cold cynic.
     I will be plain too. If he have no coat
     I'th' herald's boots, I say again the better;
     His kindred shall not awe me with a statue
     Wanting a nose or ear of his great family,
     Though they swear 'twas John-a-Gaunt's. My father was
     A soldier, and for that my mother lov'd him,
     His title of an earl was no charm to her.
     And when I find a perfect and a poor one,
     Still take me with you, cousin – if a soldier –

[9] This love-duel motif is analyzed in John Harrington Smith, *The Gay
Couple in Restoration Comedy* (Cambridge, Mass., 1948). In addition this
motif is discussed in some detail in two studies on dramatists who influenced Davenant: John Harold Wilson, *The Influence of Beaumont and
Fletcher on Restoration Drama* (Columbus, 1928); Robert Stanley Forsythe,
The Relation of Shirley's Plays to the Elizabethan Drama (New York,
1914).

Joyn: There are few of 'em rich.
Love: I have the better choice then.
    That perfect poor one I will make my husband;
    It is resolv'd! I'll tell thee more ere long, wench. (IV, 131-132)

To be sure, this clarity of mind in a female contemplating matrimony was not unheard of before. Lillia Bianca in *The Wild Goose Chase*, by Beaumont and Fletcher, is just one example of an earlier stage heroine who was perfectly frank in expounding her private views of marriage. But again, such behavior is more consistent with the dramatic heroines after the Restoration. Certainly her lack of concern for the scandal her unorthodox behavior is causing would be better related to one of Congreve's ladies. It is in "freedom and mirth" that she hears Joynture relate the various motives attributed to her desire to remain a maid. When her "main end" is said "to be kiss'd to the purpose in the gun-room / Upon a cannon by a rough commander, / Then brought to bed in his cabin of two boys", this lighthearted lady teasingly replies, "This may be" (IV, 131). To be sure, if a woman is to suffer the circulation of such injurious reports to her reputation, she is going to make it worthwhile. And this Lady Loveright does. When Warwell comes to give evidence of having satisfied her wishes, she proves that she drives a hard bargain:

Love: When I know
    How the conditions are perform'd on your part,
    You may hear further.
War: You enjoin'd me, madam,
    As I prefer'd th' enjoying you before
    My lands, or dearer studies, to appear,
    A man possest of nothing but my hopes,
    In being your creature, to deserve your favour.
Love: 'Tis true, I did, nor will I have my husband
    Borrow addition but from my self;
    Nay, he must part with what he call'd his own,
    If he would be the master of what's mine.
War: I have obey'd your will, and that you may
    Receive me as the subject of your pleasure,
    My money's vanish'd; for, by your fair hand,
    I have not one small piece of the King's coin,
    Nor care to get it. Now I shall not tempt you,

Like an Alderman-widower, with showing you
The thousand pound bags in my counter, mortgages,
Or statutes of poor debtors. I have freed all,
And sold my books too; to serve you shall be
My only study. If you search my pockets
And find the Tale of Troy, or an Almanack there,
Or William Wisdom's metres, yet renounce me.
I have no trunks of clothes; you see my wardrobe.
And if you do not now new rig me,
I have vow'd in this to be extremely lousey,
Rather than I'll cross your humour.

Love: This is a good Imprimis
Of your obedience; but you have lands yet,
And those may make you proud, and nourish hopes
You may command me.

War: They shall be all employ'd
To pious uses, sell some part of them
And build an hospital, I'll assure the rest
For the maintenance of maim'd soldiers, and that
It may appear 'twas not vain glory, or
Ambition in me of an after name,
You shall be writ the Foundress. What would you more?

Love: I would have you a perfect soldier. Without that
The rest is nothing.

War: I come now from sea,
And I have serv'd at land, for how many years;
Would you have me prentice to the trade?

Love: Till you turn a right and good one; 'tis not roaring
Or fighting for my glove can make you such.
I would have you rise up to command an army
By brave desert, not favour. In my cabinet
I have the character of a true soldier,
Writ with my father's hand; when you are such
As he describes him, I'll forbear to be
A mistress, and acknowledge you my master.
So, once more, welcome!   (IV, 155-156)

There is no softness here. Like the brilliant females in the comedies
of Etherege, Wycherley, and Congreve, Lady Loveright, eschewing all sentiment, and calculating with a clear mind, knows exactly
what she wants, and she aims to get it.

Before leaving this analysis of the influences upon Davenant in
his comic characterizations, it is necessary to mention the "char-

acter books" that were immensely popular in the early seventeenth century. In such works it was common practise to describe the character, not as an individual, but as a member of a class. The dramatists in appropriating such literary sketches for their own use tended to allow the general type characteristics to remain while infusing a few more individual attributes. It might be a very pithy example that forbad individualizing, as in Richard Brome's *The Sparagus Garden,* a play also acted in 1635:

Gil: And what's the price of this feast boy?
Boy: Plaist ill Monsieur.
Gil: What art thou a French-man?
Boy: No, I tooke you for one sir, to bargaine for your meate be-
         fore you eate it, that is not the generous English fashion, you
         shall know anon sir.   (III, iv)

More often it was considerably lengthened, as in Seawit's description of Sir Furious Inland:

Sea: He's a gentleman
         Of fair descent, and ample means, but subject
         To their disease of quarrelling; his sword
         Hangs still too near his right hand, he loves fighting
         Above all pleasures, and is more delighted
         With the dangers of a duel, than the honour
         Of having had the better; he was trusted
         By some of his noble kinsmen to my care,
         In hope the discipline of the war might tame him:
         I have done little good upon him yet,
         His metal will not bow. But surely, madam,
         Had he been present, he had paid these roarers
         In their own coin; yet thus much I can say in his defence,
         In the height of all his wildness
         He loves and honours ladies; for whose service
         He's still a ready champion.   (IV, 129)

Irrespective of the length, however, these passages were always used to exhibit the dramatist's wit. Their resulting effect, being close to caricature, would usually be mirth-provoking.

   The chief merit of this play, as with *The Wits,* is the skill whereby Davenant portrays the life of the time. Here, however, some of his local color is not so original, being traced to other comedies. For instance, when Cable and Topsail quarrel over their relative abilities as suitors for a lady's attention, Cable is quite insulting:

Cab: Better parted, why sir?
Cause you have richer suits? My observation
Hath told me hitherto, that your best parts are
A little singing out of tune, and that,
With a scurvy hoarse voice, to a fiddler's boy,
That never was admitted to a tavern,
Shall out-do you in a tap-house for a test,
When your throat is clearest. 'Tis said you can dance, too!
Caper, and do tricks like a jack-a-napes:
A prime and courtlike virtue, which you learn'd from
The dancing-schools' usher, or his underling.   (IV, 127)

It is in quite a different tone, though the subject is similar, that Iacomo, an angry Captain with a strong inferiority complex, discourses with Fabritio in Beaumont and Fletcher's *The Captain:*

Iac: You may thrive, Sir
Thou are young and handsom yet, and well enough
To please a Widow; thou canst sing, and tell
These foolish love-tales, and indite a little,
And if need be, compile a pretty matter,
And dedicate it to the honourable,
Which may awaken his compassion,
To make ye Clark o'th' Kitchen, and at length
Come to be married to my Ladies Woman,
After she's crackt i'th' Ring.   (II, i)

This tone of rather sad resentment is adopted later in the Davenant play when Cable, alone, voices the same thoughts:

Sure this lady's honest! Or if she be not
There's but small advantage to my hopes, whilst that
Tempter, young Topsail, hovers near her eye.
The rogue has qualities for love, which I want.
Why he will sing you like any widow's daughter
That's working of bone-lace; no weaver at
His loom comes near him; and dance till he tire
All the tabours in a wake. Now the truth is
I cannot sing, for with eating
Butter, when I lay amongst

> The dutch ships at Delph, my voice is quite gone;
> And for matter of dancing, you may expect as much
> From a lobster on a fishmonger's stall.
> I would the wind would turn ...   (IV, 134)

Though one would hesitate to see any influence here, the relationship is undeniable. Naturally, the subject of courting is always timely, and when described as it is here, it presents a reality to the procedure of the period that gives the play more depth.

Early in the play when the Widow Carrack is giving her maid Smoothall some sound advice on raising her personal estate, she claims,

> I may make thee a gentlewoman, though thy mother
> Was Goody Smoothall, and do it by my lord's pattent
> When I am a baroness: 'tis now in fashion
> To metamorphose chambermaids. The King
> Dubs knights, and new-stampt honour creates gentry.
>   (IV, 117-118)

Such comment is sufficient to illustrate the havoc in Caroline society when class distinctions were not rigidly observed. But it was a phenomenon noticed before. In *Volpone* the following dialogue occurs between the officious Sir Politic Would-be and the astute Peregrine:

Pol: Now, by my spurs, the symbol of my knighthood ...
Per: (aside) Lord, how his brain is humbled for an oath. (IV, ii)

According to a footnote to the play by Hazelton Spencer, this is a derisive allusion to the cheapening of the order by King James' creation of many new knights. Evidently the same problem continued, for in *The Comical Revenge: or, Love in a Tub* Etherege refers to the cheapening of knighthood in Cromwell's time, when Betty, the servant girl, refers to Sir Nicholas Cully as "'Tis one of Oliver's Knights, Madam, Sir Nicholas Cully; his Mother was my Grandmother's Dairy maid" (V, ii). From such evidence as is shown here, one might assume that the debasing of titles and honors was serious in the seventeenth century; otherwise it is unlikely that three playwrights, writing in different reigns, would find like cause to comment.

The question puzzling scholars as to Davenant's religious views might be answered somewhat in the episode concerning Sir Solemn Trifle and his Intelligencers. By allying Zeal and Scarecrow with quidnunc Trifle and having them spout the absurd anti-papal news that he promulgates, one notes Davenant's hostility towards Puritanism. It is a hostility that he can keep checked in a vein of whimsical ridicule as could Jonson when he portrayed Ananias and Tribulation Wholesome, two Puritan types in *The Alchemist*. Also it is a hostility common to courtiers of his time. Surely it was not so common to the public audience for which this play was designed, even though the strictest Puritans would not be in the playhouse. Undoubtedly this explains the indirectness with which this bit of local feeling is injected.

Certainly the most felicitous passages of local color are Davenant's own. Soon after the play begins Topsail, in jest, deplores the weaknesses of youth and so provides insight into a homely scene:

Top: 'Tis true, to these unpleasant hazards
Riot and youth must bring us:
The gallant humour of the age, no remedy.
Whilst yet the mother's blessing quarrels and chimes
Ith' pocket thus: the thrift of thirty years
Sav'd out of mince pies, butter, and dry'd hops.
It must away; but where? In the metropolis,
London, the sphere of light and harmony;
Where still your tavern bush is green and flourishing,
Your punk dancing in purple,
With music that would make a hermit frisk
Like a young dancer on a rope ... (IV, 112-113)

Later in the play Seawit, annoyed by the jealousy of two women, forsakes his gallantry and denounces them severely:

Sea: Were you never beaten? never for stealing
Conserves? Never swaddled for losing your
Sleeve silk, or making your work foul at tent-stitch?
Never for picking plums out of mince-pies,
Or breaking o' your lutes through negligence?
Had neither of you an old grandmother
With a short ebon staff, that us'd to beat you
For these faults? Sure, had you been ever beaten
You would not dare to use me thus. (IV, 180)

Such mischief as this is harmless, indeed, as compared to that of a male roustabout, pictured at the close of the play when Cable warns Sir Furious Inland:

Cab: You cub, I'll make you feel
You are not now amongst your tenants' sons,
Swaggering at a wake, in your own village,
Or stealing away a May-pole from your neighbours;
But with such men, as if you dare but scratch,
Can pare your nails to the stumps, and spoil
your clawing.   (IV, 196)

Given these contacts with the homely realities of Davenant's day, the spectator is made aware of the past as well as the present of these personages, and so their presence in the play takes on an increased reality. And with reality comes vitality.

With incidents of intrigue, a plentiful supply of humor characters, and distinct with Restoration foreshadowings, *News from Plymouth* turns out to be, in the main, a social comedy. The central plot, if it might be called a plot, is concerned with the conflict of the sexes, the basic attraction/antagonism between male and female that is always good for a laugh. In this conflict one assumes that a certain standard of behavior, a certain social ethos, exists. Adherence to it promises success. Divergence from it when treated seriously might spell tragedy. Treated lightly, it is comic. Cable is the best example of this departure from the norm. He revolts against any thought of marriage, against any suggestion of legitimate sex. Woman must rescue him from his folly, and being man's superior in the Shavian sense, she may use any method necessary, the low tactics of her opponent/suitor being the most profitable. Thus the Widow Carrack's absurd masquerade as a whore is most acceptable to us, since this is the sort of woman Cable wants. The fact that her goal is respectable is known to us but not to Cable, and thus it provides the comic irony that so tartly seasons this play.

Basically such social comedy is internal. It looks on the inside of the conflict, analyzing, mainly through speeches, the reasons for such conflict, the causes of one's separation from accepted standards. Wit is the purest type of comedy that results from it, for through it one is aware still that the incongruities are chiefly mental. Thought processes, being juxtaposed, do not unite but rather collide. Verbally, sparks result. Thus Seawit upbraids two jealous women in a passage already quoted, or again he assails a woman for prying into his affairs:

Joy: 'Tis very strange! One question more,
        And then you have leave to censure my manners.
        Pray, what estate have you?
Sea: D'you take me for a lawyer, or a citizen?
Joy: For neither.
Sea: I know none in these times
        Have or can get estates, but they! We soldiers
        Account estates but transitory things
        And can shew text for it.
Joy: Have you none, sir?
Sea: Yes! Now I think on't,
        After the death of an old aunt, I have
        The toll of a wharf near Rotherithe will
        Yield me about four marks a year.
Joy: These are but narrow blessings to entail
        Upon your heirs male. But now, sir, I hope
        I shall a little comfort your long sufferings.
        How much would you esteem your self oblig'd
        Unto that woman should redeem you from
        These wants, and danger of the war, and take
        You to her lawful bed, there furnish you
        With sleep, and peaceful thoughts; but when you wake
        Shew you her cabinets, and chests, shining
        With jewels, and with gold; that may maintain
        These joys still fresh and new?
Sea: Good, very good!
        I was never jeer'd by a smock before.
Joy: Are you struck dumb? What fair appliances
        And love might such a woman merit from
        Your tongue and heart?
Sea: First, I would fain know where that woman breathes
        That can deserve a man like me. Suppose
        She be a virgin; alas! poor green thing, what
        Is she good for? why to steal gooseberries,
        And eat young apricocks in May, before
        The stones are hard. Or pick the mortar from
        An aged wall, and swallow it most greedily.

Joy: If mirth be all your wealth, sir, it were good
        You us'd it sparingly!
Sea: But for your wealth, 'tis no more than a hermit's,
        Compar'd with a soldier's hopes. Imagine now
        The wind stands fair, we hoist up sail, we meet
        A Persian junk, or Turkish carrack, board her,
        Take her, and, in her, force a Bashaw prisoner,
        That hath a diamond in his turband, weighs,
        Let me see, about six ounces!
Joy: Would the Bashaw
        Were here, captain, though lodg'd in the major's house.
Sea: I would you were among your smooth curl'd suitors
        That have little beard, and less brain, that have
        Estates, and are fit to be jeer'd. You think
        Y'are mistress of a fine wit; go! go home!
        And keep it warm.
Joy: Methinks y'are angry, sir.
Sea: Be sure you eat no philberts, nor green cheese,
        They'll make you short-winded, and so you'll lose
        Your fine conceits for want of words to utter 'em.
                                          (IV, 158-159)

Sometimes such a wit-combat, the above being only an example of middling value, degenerates into jeering, usually a quarrel in the course of which the parties malign each other unkindly, perhaps scurrilously. Jeering is approached in a scene when Loveright, jealous of Joynture's rivalry, orders her to leave her household. As the ferocity of vocal tones become emphasized, the value of the words diminishes. The spectator takes new interest in these noisy outpourings of an emotionalized being since they might lead to vigorous physical action. When such jeering occurs, the internal comedy is becoming external.

It is this external comedy, seen in various gradations of force, that generates most of the laughter in this play. The humors lend themselves to such treatment admirably. Talkative Trifle, who provides both kinds of comedy, is chiefly humorous in his drunk scene, where his ridiculous behavior betrays the type of person he fancies himself. Thus we laugh at his external actions, made more amusing by our knowledge of what he fancies himself to be. Here external and internal comedy meet. But with Sir Furious Inland the comedy is all external. As he blusters about, assigning himself as a second to both opponents in a duel or wildly kissing his own enemy for promising to fight, it is his physical gusto, expended so absurdly, that delights us. As with most humors, it is the automatism in his nature that identifies his character so vividly. He never disappoints us, always doing what is expected of him. And because such automatism could become monotonous, the playwright places this character into a series of farcical situations. Even outrageous buffoonery, as being banged on the head with a liquor can, is not too ludicrous an act for such a fellow.

Considering the fact that *News from Plymouth* has a goodly share of inner comedy, always arresting and often a social corrective, and a vigorous portion of rowdy farce, not to forget the additions of songs and music, one might well question the reason for the play's failure. To hazard a guess is necessary, since no explanation is on record. To provide a "medley of things" in order to divert a plebeian audience was probably judicious, but to provide simultaneously only the slightest pretension to a unified plot was equally unwise. Act Three, in brief summary, might be cited as an example of the complexity of incident:

a. Bumble and Warwell are drinking with sailors when Seawit and Inland enter, the latter bristling for a fight.

b. Carrack enters disguised as a whore with Porter disguised as a squire.

c. Topsail, a drunken Trifle, and Musicians enter. Topsail serenades the ladies until they enter. After some bizarre behavior on Trifle's part, Seawit and Sir Furious enter, the latter vowing his services to the ladies' cause. Cable and Topsail enter and begin arguing, thus arousing intervention of Sir Furious. Nightingale, Loveright's servant, enters with letter. All leave in groups for various reasons.

d. Loveright has interview with Warwell.

e. Seawit and Joynture argue.

Thus one might say there are five scene changes in one act, with several scenes in themselves being occupied with a stage full of lively interplay. Act Five is even more complicated, and the first three acts are hardly less so. Such a frenetic shifting of story line is

too frequent ever to focus fully the spectator's interest. His attention is diverted so often that he soon loses any sense of dramatic
direction. The resulting frustration would inevitably prevent from
being really enjoyed that which alone would seem comical. Davenant had evidently not learned that variety in drama, when too
various, does not necessarily spice the Comic Muse.

THE PLAYHOUSE TO BE LET

It was seventeen years before Davenant was to try his hand at
another original comedy. Though he had written comic elements
in tragedies and tragicomedies during the interval, he had not
attempted a play that was dominated by the Comic Spirit. When
he did it again, actually it was only a playlet, a mere fifth act in a
program of composite bills.

The summer of 1663, being unusually warm, magnified the
headache that usually besets theatre managers at such a season.
Hordes of Londoners left for the coolness of the country, aban-
doning the theatres to the less sophisticated and less financially
fortunate. To attract them to a crowded theatre on a hot day, a
producer must have material that will be exceptionally diverting.
One can not ask an audience to think under such conditions; one
can only hope to present that which will keep the audience from
thinking how senseless it is to be in such a place at such a time.
Davenant seized the idea of capitalizing on the problem. Collecting
four different types of dramatic pieces, all brief in length, that he
had written earlier, he arranged them loosely into a composite
program, prefacing them with an extended Induction, and titled it
The Playhouse to be Let.[10]

Act One pictures the theatre, undoubtedly the Lincoln's Inn
Fields theatre, in just such a sorry state. Except for a Tire-woman

---

[10] Nethercot, Sir William D'Avenant, *Poet Laureate and Playwright-
Manager* (Chicago, 1938), p. 377, footnote 25. "Though the license fee of
The Play-house to be Let was not paid until November 3, 1663 (Adams,
p. 138), internal evidence suggests that it may have been acted slightly
earlier."

and Char-woman, one of whom is shelling beans and the other sewing, it is empty until they are immediately joined by a Player and House-keeper. While discussing their tribulations, they interview a variety of applicants for the use of the building. Four they accept, and the next four acts are devoted to their presentations. A French company presents in painstakingly broken English a translation of Molière's *Sganarelle ou le Cocu Imaginaire*. Act Three consists of Davenant's four-year-old opera *The History of Sir Francis Drake*, a "Heroique story in Stilo Recitativo". This is followed by a pageant, *The Cruelty of the Spaniards in Peru*. Act Five, the most favored in this play and the only part to be popularly accepted, is a burlesque of the Antony and Cleopatra story, not only Davenant's first original comedy in seventeen years, but, of greater importance, the introduction of burlesque drama to the Restoration stage.[11]

The idea of such a dramatic anomaly is not new. Schelling's research reveals several such productions in the late sixteenth century.[12] Still it is undoubtedly the structure of the later *Four Plays in One* by Beaumont and Fletcher that directly influenced Davenant. This piece is composed of two comedies, one tragedy, and one moral, all presented in honor of the nuptials of Emanuel, king of Portugal and Castile. Aside from a relationship in structure and a certain amount of dumbshow and pageantry, there is little else that resembles *The Playhouse to be Let*. It is much more stylized and artificial in language and dramatic development, it lacks the earthy, contemporary realism characteristic of parts of the later piece, and in comedy there is nothing so comic as the "tragedie travestie" that superbly concludes Davenant's summer showing.

Short theatrical pieces would have been familiar to many in Davenant's audience, certainly for those who remained in London during the Interregnum. Under the Puritan regime with the theatres officially closed, it was impossible for any theatrical troupe, necessarily *sub rosa*, to develop or maintain a repertory of

[11]   A brief analysis of this composite production is to be found in Dane Farnsworth Smith, *Plays About the Theatre in England from The Rehearsal in 1671 to the Licensing Act in 1737* (New York, 1936), pp. 1-8.
[12]   Felix Schelling, *Elizabethan Drama 1558-1642* (Boston, 1908), I, 401.

five act plays. Instead, wtih a minimum of actors, properties and costumes, they presented what were termed "drolls".[13] These drolls were usually farcical fragments from established plays, such as the Bottom episode from *A Midsummer Night's Dream*. Then, too, they might be entirely original. Practically always they were comical, since tragedy does not lend itself so effectively to such brief treatment. And brief they must be, for at the approach of Roundhead constabulary, an easy flight was desirable. After years of seeing such drolls in surreptitious performance, one would surely feel nostalgic at a performance of the Antony and Cleopatra burlesque, which is akin in size and spirit.

The first act of *The Playhouse to be Let* reassures us that Davenant, in his use of local color, has not lost his touch. In fact, the chief value of this act lies in its vivid presentation of theatrical conditions in the early years of the Restoration. We meet the professional amateurs who have a new mode of entertainment that will revolutionize the theatre, a perpetual plague of theatre managers in any age. We learn that the Red Bull Theatre has "no tenants in it but old spiders". We are told of the sideshow entertainers of the time, of "the old gentlewoman / That professes the galliard on the rope; Another rare Turk that flies without wings." We are informed of the rapidity with which London is growing:

> Brainford's the place!
> Perhaps 'tis now somewhat too far i' th' suburbs;
> But the mode is for builders to work slight and fast;
> And they proceed so with new houses,
> That old London will quickly overtake us.   (IV, 21)

But most fascinating of all is the insight allowed us of the more colorful theatre-goers at a summer performance, such as the one-handed fat man who claps at every play by belaboring his plump cheek. In addition, the methods used to assure a hearty reaction to the play are quite enlightening. A dozen laundry-maids are to be hired because, having developed tough hands from clapping linen, they will be able to provide a loud noise that will provoke

[13] Leo Hughes, *A Century of English Farce* (Princeton, 1956), p. 23 *passim*.

a general applause. Perhaps the shrewdest trick of all is also one
of the oldest:

> We must provide our party 'gainst tomorrow;
> Watch at the doors before the play begins,
> And make low congèes to the cruel critics
> As they come in . . .   (IV, 33)

The comedy that exists in this Act is mainly provided by the
speaker of the above advice, the Player. Laughter would, of
course, be invoked by the accent of the French troupe's representative and some of the nationalistic comments made, a method we
have seen Davenant using before, but it is for the tart-tongued
Player that the author has provided the best lines of dialogue.
From the very beginning of the scene his dry wit is evident. A
loud knock at the door inspires him to identify it as "some university muse is in hard labour / And she takes our Tire woman for a
midwife". Cases for musical instruments he calls "A load of tombs
for dead fiddles". As to be expected, such cleverness occasionally
invites a sharp retort:

> Your wit, sir, will never grow up to madness;
> 'Tis only the fume of an empty stomach.
> You may recover in the Term, when you
> Get money to get meat.   (IV, 21-22)

To be sure, his singing voice is not very pleasant, provoking the
musician to remark, ". . . and your voice does breed some doubt /
Of your virginity." But his speaking voice is excellent, one can be
sure, and he avails himself of every opportunity to use it in the
sort of speeches that depend on mannered vocal inflections. With
this Player, Davenant depicts a common theatrical type, one who
amuses for brittle sophistication and an endless volley of acrid
repartee. Unfortunately, the role of this fellow is all too short, for
the comedy that he provides, basically mental, is a comedy Davenant provides less than one would wish. Considering his summer
audience, however, such brevity was probably a result of the playwright-manager's business intuition.

The historical value of this theatrical hodgepodge lies in the
burlesque of the Antony and Cleopatra story. Burlesque was to

have an honorable tradition in the English theatre after 1660. One instantly thinks of Buckingham's *The Rehearsal*, Fielding's *Tom Thumb*, and Sheridan's *The Critic*. One is not likely to think of this little playlet of Davenant; nevertheless, Davenant was the Restoration innovator of this genre. Burlesque in method is much like farce, both genres making use of the extravagant, the exaggerated, and even the grotesque. Both exploit the physical. The essential difference, however, is that the sole aim of farce is to entertain. On the other hand, burlesque's intent is to criticize. First burlesque imitates, and then it ridicules. In doing so it is never violent or angry, as satire can be; rather it always strives to incite laughter.[14] Yet its *raison d'être* is something disliked.

The something disliked by Davenant was the vogue for classical travesty, a type of drama depicting ancient history that revelled in bombastic heroics. The fact that he started this trend with his own heroic drama did not dissuade Davenant from disliking the excesses to which it had developed. The most recent success of this sort was a translation of Corneille's *Pompey* by "the matchless Orinda", Mrs. Katherine Philips. First performed on February 10, 1662/63 in Dublin, it was immediately hailed by spectators, who were enraptured by the gorgeous costumes, flamboyant scenery, inflated eloquence, heroic songs, and stately dances.[15] Immensely praised, it was put into print, and its author became the most lauded poetess of her time. Acutely conscious of how his heroic drama had degenerated, Davenant resolved to sharpen audience sensibilities, even if it be only a summer audience. Therefore, he took the same story, and with a comic purpose he out-travestied Orinda's serious travesty.[16]

The semblance of plot that exists is entirely without point. Following a sort of dumbshow to introduce the celebrities and a dance of "the Gypsies with which Cleopatra entertain'd Caesar",

---

[14] Victor Clinton Clinton-Baddeley, *The Burlesque Tradition in the English Theatre after 1660* (London, 1952), p. 2.

[15] Philip Webster Souers, *The Matchless Orinda* (Cambridge, Mass., 1931), p. 185.

[16] According to Souers (pp. 204-205) Langbaine mentions seeing Davenant's travesty acted by itself at the end of Orinda's translation at Dorset Garden.

both included to parody the theatrical trappings of a serious classical travesty, the Player calls for "the burlesquers / That show the
wrong side of the hero's outward". Two of Ptolemy's Eunuchs
enter, and from then on the various ennobled personages appear
solely in order to be torn from their pedestals. In our own century
George Bernard Shaw has performed a similar theatrical phenomenon with some of history's more famed personalities in order to
give them an appearance of reality. To do this he portrays them
as common mortals who are possessed by the usual petty foibles
that beset the ordinary man. Davenant goes much further, however. Here he completely debases his historical figures until they
resemble humanity at its lowest common denominator.

Cleopatra, Mark Antony, and Caesar are revealed to us through
the narratives of others as well as by their own speeches and actions. The Eunuchs, who discuss Cleopatra as Enobarbus does in
Shakespeare's version, refer to their queen as a "black Gypsy" and
her famous lover as "trusty Tony" who is "so hard of heart that it
is held all boney". Even dignified, elderly Caesar is said to have
"comes a caterwawling". When servants are so devoid of respect
for their own masters, we naturally expect that the masters' presence will be somewhat less glamorous than legend fondly affirms.
Our expectations are more than justified. Cleopatra is both coy
and crude. Caesar's threatening of her Eunuch stimulates the following rejoinder:

> Is this you Caesar? tell, me dearest bunting:
> I'faiks I must have leave to speak of one thing.
> Can he that's cock of Rome be so mistaken
> As thus to threaten poor Egyptian capon?
> I scorn, though but a female and no Roman,
> To meddle with an Eunuch who is no man.
> When first we saw you sailing to our haven,
> We little thought to find your cock a craven.
>
> (IV, 97)

Carrying on this animal imagery that is anything but flattering,
Antony warns her:

> Peace, lamb; and be, like lamb-kine, meek and humble,
> Caesar, like wolf, will bite when he does grumble.

Shortly afterwards, when the domestic harmony is in danger, Caesar himself finds occasion for an animal simile:

> Shall lovers fall to scratch like midnight pusses?
> Let's turn their frowns and wrath lo leers and busses. (IV, 98)

Is this the love on which the fate of two continents hinged? Hardly! When Antony can address Cleopatra as "Chuck" and playfully accuse her of "wear[ing] the breeches", he is no longer the dauntless Roman hero, much less a dashing lover. Davenant could do little more to ridicule history. Yet he does it. At the conclusion of the playlet, following a brief verbal brawl between the slatternly queen and Pompey's widow, an episode that anticipates a similar one in Dryden's *All for Love*, all prepare to go to an alehouse, where, according to Caesar, the tapsters know him. And their friendship is vitally necessary, for our two heroes are financially broke. Caesar has spent his money on the war while Antony's plunder, by his own admission, "is squander'd with girls, and I'm forced now to borrow".

Despite the absurdity of these characterizations, they would not be nearly so titillating were it not for the dialogue. Davenant has used the heroic couplet, undoubtedly because it was familiar as the favorite form for tragedy, and twisted it in order to mock. To do this he has made liberal use of feminine end-rhymes and forced rhymes, and in doing so he often juxtaposes the most incongruous ideas:

Nimp: There Tony is our Cleopatra leading;
      Her eyes look blue; pray heav'n she be not breeding! (IV, 96)
Ptol: I am as surely he, most mighty Tony
      As she is my sweet sister, and your honey. (96)
Ptol: Of which even Pompey muncht his share in cabin,
      Where, from the shore, he beckon'd many a drab in:
      Under the rose I speak't, he was a dragon
      When he brown damsel got with scarce a rag on. (97)
Anth: Caesar, things are not as th' world now supposes;
      The case seems plain as on your face your nose is. (98)

On occasion this end rhyme can cross speeches as when Caesar ends a speech with "Mass! now I think on't, 'tis Pompey's rich widow" and immediately Antony begins his with "Of mumping minx would we were fairly rid, ho!" (IV, 99). Some of these examples also show that alliteration is another technical device Davenant employs to heighten the ludicrous speech.

Allied with this burlesque accentuation of rhyme is the trick, well known to our comedians today, of not saying what has been expected, particularly if the allusion is somewhat obscene. Caesar, in decrying Cleopatra's eunuch, indulges in this:

> With blood of Roman your Eunuch does grow fat;
> Such knaves wax cruel, having lost – you know what. (IV, 97)

Like laughter can be invoked by the incorporation of a popular maxim. After Antony ends a speech with the word "forage", Cleopatra quips, "Caesar may spare his breath to cool his porridge" (IV, 98). George Bernard Shaw, who knew the value of the maxim in his debunking of heroes and heroic attitudes, uses the same maxim as quoted above in his own *Caesar and Cleopatra*.[17] Though this maxim has been traced back to sixteenth-century England [18] and has even appeared in such foreign works as the writings of Rabelais [19] and Plutarch,[20] it might be more than a coincidence that this same maxim should appear in both comic versions of the Cleopatra story. One likes to think that Shaw consulted this slight travesty before writing his own major comedy.

It would be over three hundred years before George Bernard Shaw would reinvigorate English comedy with some of the same methods Davenant uses here. Though this little burlesque is all but forgotten today, it was not ignored in its own time. Exclusive of the other sections of *The Playhouse to be Let*, it reaped considerable popularity, justly deserved for its vigorous comic force. It is no wonder that Buckingham was to appropriate its type for his own disparagement of certain dramatists. That Davenant himself was one of those lampooned in *The Rehearsal* is one of the ironies of theatre history. However, Davenant, doubtlessly, would have

---

[17] George Bernard Shaw, *Caesar and Cleopatra*, II.
[18] *A New Dictionary of Quotations on Historical Principles from Ancient and Modern Sources*, ed. H. L. Mencken (New York, 1942), p. 126.
[19] *Familiar Quotations*, ed. John Bartlett, 13th ed. (Boston, 1955), p. 60b.
[20] *Hoyt's New Cyclopedia of Practical Quotations*, compiled by Kate Louise Roberts (New York, 1947), p. 709.

overlooked the cruel jibe could he have known what an illustrious dramatic genre he had introduced to the Restoration stage.

A brief reappraisal of the only three original comedies penned by Davenant sees them as two hits and a miss. He missed in *News from Plymouth* for his inability to maintain clarity in his plotting. Otherwise in that play, as in the others, he impresses us with his considerable verbal dexterity, his sense of the ridiculous, and his feeling for homely realities. Already he appears capable of writing fine comedy. Yet if one is to evaluate properly his skill in dramatizing the Comic Spirit, it is necessary to analyze his way of putting it to work in tragedy and tragicomedy, a real test for a playwright of the seventeenth century. Following this analysis in the next chapter, our understanding of Davenant's contribution will be closer to completion.

IV

COMEDY IN DAVENANT'S TRAGEDIES AND TRAGICOMEDIES

> Pure Wit, like ingots wrought without allay,
> Will serve for hoard, but not for common pay.
> Th' allay's coarse metal makes the finer last;
> Which else would in the peoples' handling waste.
> So country jigs and farces mixt among
> Heroic scenes make plays continue long.

The above excerpt from the Prologue to the Restoration revival of Davenant's most successful comedy, *The Wits,* expresses the author's attitude towards the admixture of farce with non-farcical material. Alter a few words and it could easily mean the blending of comedy with non-comical, even tragic, material. With this re-interpretation Davenant would also agree. Like his English predecessors and contemporaries, he had no objection to mixing the genres. Whether or not he had talent in mixing them is another question.

The fundamental purpose of introducing comedy into a serious play is for the spectator's emotional relief. Without such episodic diversion, the accumulating tensions generated by a tragedy would quite likely become too oppressive to be tolerable. With such episodic diversion, the spectator's emotional feelings are offered release in laughter, permitting a temporary purgation which, in contrast, will serve to heighten the impact of the tragedy to follow. Simple as this may sound, it is not with equal ease that playwrights practise this principle. If unskilled, they might insert a comic interval that appears to have no more value than the separation of two incidents which could not be presented in immediate succession. Or again the comic element might seem merely to

shorten a long lapse of time. To avoid such an offence, the polished playwright will smoothly integrate the comic portion so that its
purpose in being present will be not only technical, but functional.

To be functional the comedy should serve to underline and
support the theme, tone, and mood emphasized in the rest of the
drama. Necessarily a proper balance between the two must be
maintained, this balance being determined by the nature of the
play itself. For instance, a tragedy would be unlikely to contain
as much comedy as a tragicomedy, for too much attention to
lighter issues would diminish the tragic force. Then, too, the
serious plot itself will decide the kind of comedy that would be
most suitable. Ideally, comedy should not only amuse but have a
didactic value as well. That is, it should unite with the tragedy to
present a unity of effect. While diverting and extending the spectator's thoughts and emotions, comedy and serious drama must
work together towards a single goal, a singleness of impression.

ALBOVINE, KING OF THE LOMBARDS

When Davenant wrote his first play, *Albovine, King of the
Lombards*,[1] a tragedy, unity of effect was evidently not so important to him as theatrical sensationalism. Based on the skull-goblet
story of King Alboinus and Queen Rosamunda, originally told by
Paul Diaconus in Book One, Chapter 27, and Book Two, Chapters 28-29, of his *De Gestis Longobardorum*,[2] it is geared to the
spectator who enjoys Shakespeare's *Othello*, Webster's gory tragedies, and the bitter satire of Marston. In fact, in both language and
plotting echoes of these plays are frequently present.

King Albovine, the Lombardian victor, infuriates his Italian
captive-wife by proposing a toast from the skull of her father
whom he has slain in battle. Previously docile, she now thirsts for

[1] Harbage, *Sir William Davenant, Poet Venturer 1606-1668* (Philadelphia,
1935), p. 222. Harbage, unlike Nethercot and all other critics of this
dramatist, argues, though with two unimpressive reasons, that *The Cruel
Brother* was Davenant's first play.
[2] Harbage, pp. 29-30. Harbage contends that Davenant's immediate
source was not Paulus but the adaptation of this story by Bandello and
then retold by Belleforest in Tome IV, Histoire 19, of *Histoires Tragiques*.

revenge. First of all, the King's catamite, Paradine, is lured, through trickery, to her bed so that he can be blackmailed into becoming an accomplice to her diabolical desire. Meanwhile Hermegild, her ambitious admirer, attempts to persuade Valdaura, the innocent bride of Paradine, to poison her faithless spouse. From here until all the principals are dead, either by their own or another's hand, an endless number of complications ensue, fraught with scenes depicting the most superlative horrors. This bloody spectacle would hardly seem congenial to any comedy but that of the most sardonic sort, and this Davenant has judiciously provided.

Grimold, a rough old Captain, and easily the most boldly drawn character in this gory drama, represents the surly old soldier whose honesty and clear judgment prevent any possible acceptance of the sham or sleek. From the very opening of the drama his perspicacity is evident. Coarse and crude, he vents his spleen in speeches that not only depict the true character of the courtiers he despises, but also serve to present a very vivid local color, particularly that concerned with sexual mores of the day. In praising the lovely Valdaura, he couches his comments rather roughly:

> ... though my obdurate sufferance
> In active war hath quite depriv'd me of
> All amorous gesture; though not these forty
> Winters have I seen any of her sex
> But suttlers' wives, who, instead of fillets,
> Wrap their sooty hair in horses' girts; though
> My marrow is frozen in my bones,
> Yet I melt before her eyes. When I see her,
> I grow proud below the navel. For she
> Is none o' th' French nursery that practise
> The sublime frisk. None o' your jigging girls,
> That perch paraquitoes on their fists,
> And ride to the Court like Venus' falconers. (I, 29-30)

When he is reminded that Albovine is in love with his queen, Grimold's crusty jest strikes at the moral license typical of marriages at the court:

> In love with his own wife! that's held incest
> In Court: variety is more luscious. (I, 52)

Sadly in need of money, with his bold petitions to the King to pay him his rightful debts seemingly in vain, he uses his crude wit to discuss the possibility of a pension that would be earned by methods obviously prevalent:

Grim: Have you not each a mistress that maintains
You in expense and riot? Hah! fame gives
It out, you smooth gallants are much obliged
Unto the sins of ladies.

Cuny: Conrade can prattle somewhat, sir, to that purpose.

Conr: Good faith, you do me wrong. I've worn, sir,
A lady's slipper in my hat, or so.
Frollo is the man that gets their pendants,
Armlets, rings, and all the toys of value.

Frol: Excuse me, sir; not I. Signor Cunymond
Has all the voice at Court. We know, sir, when
And where a certain duchess, sir; –
You copulate with titles, you.
The heralds are your bawds.

Cuny: Hold! grow particular in such a theme as this!

Grim: Well, gentlemen, I must be furnish'd too.

Cuny: With a mistress?

Grim: Yes, enquire me out some old land-carack.
I am content to stretch my loins for a pension.

Cuny: At what rate do you value yourself?

Grim: I was never pawn'd, sir.

Cuny: How, captain!

Grim: In this lean age we value all things
According to the rate they pawn for.

Frol: But we must know how much you would receive
In price of your activity?

Conr: You must never stray after fresh pasture.

Grim: Some eight; ay, ay, eight hundred crowns a-year will do't.
I am desirous of no more, than will
Maintain my genet and my dwarf.

Cuny: Your excuse procur'd, 'tis fit you now tell,
How far in your defence I may engage
My honour: is not your flesh a little tainted!
Are you not unwholesome?

Grim: O death, no; no, no, no! Do not think I have
A conscience so ill-bred to put myself
Upon a lady, when unfit for the affair.

Cuny: Well, captain, now with your own eyes survey
Your limbs; what use can a lady have

Of you? to propagate the cough o' th' lungs?
Frol: Or beget cripples to people an hospital?
Conr: Or produce another nation that may
Wage fierce battle 'gainst the cranes?
Grim: Yet I can follow your bodies with rough
Motion, and not shed my limbs by the way –
Cuny: I told ye he'ld make a jest on't.
Grim: But I will kick ye in earnest, – kick ye
For my exercise and warmth, till my toes
Grow crooked –   (I, 52-54)

Unhealthy as this satire seems to be, still it is in tune with the tone of corruption that pervades the play. In the tradition of Shakespeare's Thersites, Grimold is a social commentator who both amuses, an uncomfortable amusement perhaps, and makes explicit the life he contemns. Grimold could well be the foul-mouthed philosopher that voices the moral of the drama. Unfortunately, this role is not consistently maintained. For the questionable rewards of a low comedy incident, Davenant jettisons this possibility.

In the fourth act, as a last resort in his petition to the king for money, Grimold dons an old rug, muffled with clouts, in order to fake old age and painful decrepitude. To the puzzled Hermegild he groans repeatedly and complains of starvation cramps. Sensing the counterfeit, Hermegild informs the king of a plan he has devised. Aware of the old soldier's amazingly "hot blood", he enlists Thesina, a court lady, as a decoy. From behind an arras they watch her tantalize the impostor until, with lascivious words and eager actions, he is about to have his lustful will. Just then Hermegild and the king appear, and the panting Grimold's plan is thwarted. Without a doubt the farcical elements of this scene are uproariously comic. "There's no fool like an old fool" is a saw that is strongly supported by the laughable downfall of this aging degenerate. But at the expense of laughter, Davenant has seriously devitalized a strong character. Perhaps the idea of the disguise is to reveal the weakness of this earthy man, the man who could with withering wit mock all others. In that he succeeds. But in making Grimold appear wholly ridiculous, Davenant has destroyed the earlier worth of his satire which had nicely balanced the opposing plot. Now in mixing the two, and none too smoothly, this balance gives way to uneven perspectives. Later in Act Five, Grimold, reinstated in the king's favor, resumes his former role as fearless critic, savagely reviling courtiers for their affectations and unnatural French airs, but it is too late to restore the original harmony. The very loudness of the laughter evoked by the temporary lapse in character consistency makes that impossible.

Other comical figures in this play are generally related to Grimold as objects of his barbed wit. Dominant among these is Cunymond, an absurdly pretentious old Courtier, who undoubtedly smells of the same perfume that adorned the dandies in Shakespeare's plays. From his first entrance, his foppish behavior pertinently illustrates the reasons for Grimold's attacks. He is vain, supercilious, and without common sense. Even the king enjoys teasing him:

Albo: Is not your name Pigwiggin?
Cuny: Pigwiggin! your Grace was wont to call me
Cunymond: I am no fairy.
Albo: Nor I the king of fairies. 'Slight, sir, d'ye
Present me with a cup made o' th' bottom
Of an acorn, or Queen Mab's thimble?
Fill me a bowl, where I may swim
And bathe my head, ...   (I, 37)

His folly, however, not only serves as a foil to Grimold but as an emotional release to the spectator. The above dialogue, possibly alluding to *A Midsummer Night's Dream,* admirably proves this. The lightness of this conversation immediately precedes the horrific scene when Albovine invites his wife to drink from her father's skull. By allowing the tension to abate temporarily, together with the incongruity of the comparison between Queen Mab's thimble and a deposed monarch's skull, the resulting shock will be further intensified.

Thesina's comedy, too, is allied with Grimold. Representative of the bawdy court ladies found in Jacobean drama, she is uncommonly free with her tongue. In the manner of Juliet's nurse, she unabashedly jests with Rhodolinda about a bride's sexual duties. Even with men she shows no modesty. In advising Paradine to be discreet in his amour with her lady so that she can sleep without sinning in wish, she remarks:

> But you young soldiers are so boisterous,
> You'll think anon y'are battering some Town-wall. (I, 62)

This very lack of ladylike subtlety would certainly succeed in shocking into laughter a sophisticated audience.

The humor of *Albovine* is strictly in the tradition of the more pessimistic Jacobean playwrights. A diseased life is being portrayed, and the only comedy that fits it is the corrupt, the grisly, even the obscene. To depict such comedy with taste is difficult, and for Davenant, a novice, it proved impossible. But the very virility of this bitter satire speaks well for his exceptional promise.

THE CRUEL BROTHER

The Cruel Brother, another Fletcherian tragedy and Davenant's next effort, had more luck than its predecessor in securing a hearing. On January 12, 1626-7, Sir Henry Herbert licensed the play, and at an unspecified later date, it was produced at "the private House, in the Blacke-Fryers: By His Maiesties Servants".[3] Any more favor than that which it might have recieved has not been recorded. Still it is doubtful if it found an eager audience, for it warrants no thoughtful recognition.

Again the plot is sordid and complex, requiring only a brief resumé in order to suggest its theme. The Duke of Siena is inflamed with a desire for the bride of his male lover, Count Lucio. Since she is supremely virtuous, he is forced to satisfy his lust by rape. The woman's brother, Foreste, who is devoted to Count Lucio, feels compelled to avenge the family stain by subjecting her to a slow yet sure death. Count Lucio joins Foreste to confront the Duke with his guilt, who, in turn, has already arranged for Foreste's murder. Suddenly repentant, the Duke hastens to withdraw his orders, and in doing so he dies in his own trap. Foreste

[3] Nethercot, *Sir William D'Avenant, Poet Laureate and Playwright-Manager* (Chicago, 1938), pp. 55-56.

and Count Lucio are also assassinated. All, while succumbing, forgive the guilt of the others.

Before his stage is strewn with the dead, Davenant has relieved the bloodshed with some desirable touches of comedy. The least successful of these, however, is Castruccio, a satirical Courtier, whose prototype has already been drawn in the person of Grimold. According to Davenant's editors this caustic gentleman is meant to satirize George Wither, their theory being based on a speech in the play that obviously alludes to Wither's work *Abuses Stript and Whipt*.[4] If this is true, then Davenant must have felt the greatest scorn for that dedicated Puritan. Castruccio is an ugly character, uglier than Grimold even, closer to Shakespeare's Thersites on whom he is certainly patterned. His sarcasm in hailing a fop as "the great minion to our Duke" (I, 143) recalls the more serious charge of "male whore" with which Thersites taunts Patroclus in *Troilus and Cressida* (V, i). And like Thersites he is generally too horribly depraved in his speech and thoughts to be comic. This man's very obsession with the evil that surrounds him chokes what wit his scornful remarks might otherwise evoke. To be witty one must be objective, and this Castruccio fails to be. The Duke himself recognizes his evil:

> He's bad enough t'infect the very Devil. (I, 164)

Moreover, the other courtiers are aware of the basic hypocrisy of this critic's satirical remarks, as the following dialogue concerning the bride's rape reveals:

Cast: What, repent! I prithee, sweet Duarte,
     Wrong not divinity so much, waste not
     A virtue that would more profit others:
     And to suppose that the lady was ravish'd
     Is an heresy, which my soul must ne'er
     Be guilty of. Do not I know, women
     Are a kind of soft wax, that will receive
     Any impression?

Duar: And do not I know, there is difference
     In workmen as in wax? Hard wax, when cold,
     Accepts of no impression. By coldness
     I infer chastity; for chastity is cold.

[4]   Davenant, I, 111-112.

Cast: But those workmen are harder far
Than that hard wax. And 'tis hardest of all
To find those workmen; unless by Russia
Where the people freeze till they spit snow. Come,
Kiss me chuck! Again! Once more!

Dor: A precious satirist! This surly dog
Inveighs 'gainst lechery in others, 'cause
He would engross all women to himself.

Cast: Your greatest thieves are commonly begot
When parents do their lechery by stealth.
Men get cowards when frighted in the act.
And by such vulgar consequence, 'tis now
A proper time to beget a pander:
One that may hereafter do to other men
The same office, which we do the Duke now.
Come! Shall we in and try?

Duar: You presume much on an easy nature
And how extravagant you are abroad
I am not so unkind to question.

Cast: Faith, wench! I've some interest in
Every child that plays i'th' street. (I, 165-166)

It would be a perverted soul, indeed, who could find much about
this man that would provoke a pleasantry.

On the other hand genuine guffaws hail the antics of two very
familiar characters, one Lothario and his rustic servant Borachio,
two "voluntary mistakes of Nature", who are tolerated at court
for the mirth their behavior provides. Lothario is a sort of court
baboon who fancies himself, quite without a reason, the Duke's
favorite. His ambition is beyond compare:

> The excrements and mere defects of nature
> Shall be reduc'd to ornaments in me.
> I'll feed upon the tongues of nightingales,
> For so each fart I let will be a song – (I, 142)

Unaware of the incongruity existing between his assumed elegance
and the natural coarseness the above speech betrays, he, like some
Restoration dandies to come, attempts to gild himself outwardly
with fine clothes and affected mannerisms. When he does pretend
dignity of speech, it is with a Tamburlainian flamboyance that is
equally ridiculous:

Not the four winds, met in March, shall cool my spleen.

(I, 158)

Quite rightly he is termed "the most resplendent fop / That ever did discredit nature" (I, 132).

His sidekick Borachio serves in contrast as another diverting type. Though a poor farmer, his vanity is his philosophical wisdom, which he continually bespeaks in an endless series of proverbs. He, too, has a goal. Lothario has promised him preferment and he will not give his master peace until he receives it, not even if it requires some physical scuffling on stage. Certainly this strange pair of fools would tempt courtiers, as they do here, to tease them unmercifully. Because they do so, a generous supply of comedy relieves the gloom.

Earlier it was mentioned that Lothario and Borachio are familiar. Similar gulls attended by witless and gullible servants appear in other plays, such as Freshwater and Gudgeon in Shirley's realistic comedy *The Ball*, which appeared a few years later.[5] But the familiarity here is far more striking than a mere resemblance in comic types. Davenant's nineteenth-century editors noted their resemblance to Cervantes' Don Quixote and Sancho Panza and mentioned it briefly in a footnote.[6] Further study of the great Spanish novel bears out this resemblance, particularly in relation to Borachio. In this play we are told that he "is / a bundle of proverbs, whom he Lothario seduc'd / From the plough to serve him for preferment" (I, 132-133). And later we learn that he has forsaken a wife in order to do so. In *Don Quixote* we read the following:

In the meanwhile Don Quixote was bringing his powers of persuasion to bear upon a farmer who lived near by, a good man – of this title may be applied to one who is poor – but with very few wits in his

[5]   Comedy and comic types are discussed in Arthur H. Nason, *James Shirley, Dramatist* (New York, 1915) and Hanson T. Parlin, *A Study in Shirley's Comedies of London Life*, doctoral dissertation (University of Pennsylvania, 1914).

[6]   Davenant, I, 146. "It has lately been suggested that Shakespeare might possibly have read *Don Quixote*; but there is really nothing to prove that he did. That D'avenant was acquainted with Cervantes may be safely inferred, for Borachio is quite an Italian Sancho Panza."

head. The short of it is, by pleas and promises, he got the hapless
rustic to agree to ride forth with him and serve him as his squire.
Among other things, Don Quixote told him that he ought to be more
than willing to go, because no telling what adventure might occur
which would win them an island, and then he would be left to be the
governor of it. And so Sancho Panza forsook his wife and children
and consented to be squire. (I, 60) [7]

The problem of providing the office for Borachio is more than
once a source of embarrassment for Lothario, whereas the latter's
counterpart, Don Quixote, is frequently reminded of the island
which he never locates. A greater source of contention for both
are the proverbs of the servants. As we have seen, Borachio favors
them. Sancho Panza also is fond of quoting them, much to the
irritation of his master:

"I should have been surprised, Sancho" said his master, "if in the
course of your speech you had not rung in some proverb." (II, 697)

Borachio, typical of his class, believes in witchcraft and believes
he is born to greatness through his star. On the other hand, Sancho
Panza reveals an abiding interest in astrology:

In God's name, sir, do me not this wrong. If your Grace will not
wholly desist from this enterprise, at least put it off until morning;
for according to that knowledge of the heavens that I acquired as a
shepherd, it should not be as much as three hours from now until
dawn, seeing that the mouth of the Horn is directly overhead and
midnight is in line with the left arm. (I, 147)

Then, too, the rustic honesty of both servants results in tactless-
ness that proves humiliating to their masters. Borachio informs
Lothario that he is the object of contemptuous laughter, while
Sancho Panza reveals that his master is also being ridiculed:

Well, in the first place, the common people look upon your Grace as
an utter madman and me as no less a fool. The "hidalgos" are saying
that, not content with being a gentleman, you have had to put a
"Don" in front of your name and at a bound have made yourself into
a "caballero", with four vinestocks, a couple of acres of land, and
one tatter ... (II, 524)

---

[7]   Samuel Putnam's very readable translation of the Cervantes' classic,
published in two volumes in 1949, was used for this study.

Similarities of this sort are more than coincidence. Davenant was definitely impressed by Cervantes' comic masterpiece.

Still struggling to integrate his comic subplot with the dominating tragic story, Davenant goes even further here in attempting to relate his "humor" characters to the tragic action. For instance, Lothario becomes involved in the murderous machinations so fully that it is he who stabs the Duke and then dies himself in a duel with another courtier. A certain plot unity is the result, to be sure, but it is a unity that cannot be justified artistically. To force it, Davenant again imposes a behavioral inconsistency upon one of his comic characters. Nothing in the previous picture of Lothario has prepared the spectator for his sudden display of bravery and his most manly death. It is with considerable difficulty that one accepts such action. We can praise Davenant for his "humors", his farcical incidents, and sometimes deadly satire, but we must admit that he is as yet unable to wed comedy to tragedy.

THE SIEGE

For his third play Davenant switched from tragedy to tragicomedy. Since he could not find audience favor with his rhetorical tragedies, he decided to try his luck with a dramatic combination of sentiment and comedy. *The Siege*, as it was called when printed in the folio of 1673, is traditionally believed to be the same drama that was licensed for the stage on July 22, 1629, under the title *The Colonel*.[8] Undoubtedly, it was revised after its original presentation, as were other Davenant dramas, but since there is no possibility of knowing where the alterations occurred, we will accept it here for study as it was printed. In any case, it was acted both before and after the Civil Wars without there being any records of its being warmly received. Whatever revisions occurred, they were evidently not beneficial in promoting a theatrical success.

The serious plot concerns the love and honor theme, which Davenant is using here for the first time. Afterwards he was rarely

[8] Harbage, p. 228.

to abandon it. Florello, a brilliant commander in the Florentine army which is besieging the city of Pisa, desperately loves the daughter of the enemy's Governor. Reluctant to lead a battery against the city as his Duke has commanded, Florello, though tormented with a sense of personal unworthiness, deserts to Pisa. There the Governor welcomes him gladly, but his daughter Bertolina does not. Horrified at the thought of his losing all honor, she upbraids him severely. Agonized by her repulse, he returns to his forces at her suggestion and aid, a deed that is to earn her father's extreme displeasure. At home Florello has no will to live, and thus he seeks his friend Soranzo to slay him. At this time he learns that his friend is also in love with Bertolina. Now, deeming her false, Florello decides to live and seek vengeance. Prodigious in battle, he storms Pisa successfully and orders the execution of his beloved. Then for a second time he weakens. Shamed by her pride, he gives Bertolina to Soranzo and implores them to kill him. Bertolina refuses to be disposed of against her own inclinations. She convinces the Florentine commander of her constant love, and Soranzo accepts the unhappy inevitable.

Actually overshadowing the above plot is the comic underplot that is concerned with the humiliations suffered by a couple of braggart soldiers. Ariotto and Lizaro are two gentlemen volunteers who delight in praising the daring and skill of each other, particularly if there is someone within hearing distance. But it is all surface bravado, for they are both in the power of a bully captain, Piracco. Evidently they have agreed to provide him with all his wants so long as he never reveals them as cowards or himself as their pensioner. But heartless Piracco is indifferent to their fine feelings and soon invites Mervole, a duellist, to share the spoils. For some time Ariotto and Lizaro spend their time futilely avoiding their tyrants while attempting to impress others. Then their hopes for freedom are temporarily lifted when Mervole and Piracco draw swords in anger. But their wish is frustrated when Piracco is downed, suffering no greater injury than the lancing of a troublesome imposthume on his leg. Meanwhile Soranzo, who has been inveigled into their affairs, agrees to a friendly duel with Mervole, and the two volunteers, much to their horror, are chosen as seconds. At this time the tide in their affairs turns. Following frantic attempts to devise methods to avoid such a duty, their worries are ended when Mervole's wrist is pricked, and he is incapacitated for further action. Swiftly taking advantage of their superior position, they imperiously denounce the disabled man. Piracco, too, is to feel their arrogance. Explaining that the lancing of his imposthume has let out his valor as well, Piracco now is loathe to endanger his sound body. Fleeced by Mervole and tormented by the two volunteers whom he formerly tormented, he is eventually demoted for his cowardice. With this bullying of the bully, all ends to the satisfaction of the others.

The character of Piracco is most certainly suggested by Fletcher's *The Humorous Lieutenant*. In that play the hero suffers from a painful wound in his side, which clearly does not undermine his courage. Rather the opposite! Leontes expresses it thus:

> ... I'll say this for him
> There fights no braver soldier under sun, gentlemen:
> Shew him an enemy, his pain's forgot straight;
> And where other men by beds and baths have ease,
> And easy rules of physic; set him in a danger,
> A danger that's a fearful one indeed,
> Ye rock him, and he will so play about ye!
> Let it be ten to one he ne'er comes off again,
> Ye have his heart; and then he works it bravely,
> And thoroughly bravely, not a pang remember'd.
> I have seen him do such things belief would shrink at. (I, i)

Later he is sufficiently wounded to require rest, and following his recovery his attitude, by his own admission, has changed considerably:

> Lord, what ail I, that I have no mind to fight now?
> I find my constitution mightily alter'd,
> Since I came home: I hate all noises too,
> Especially the noise of drums. I am now as well
> As any living man; why not as valiant?
> To fight now, is a kind of vomit to me;
> It goes against my stomach.　　　　　(II, iv)

In order to avoid going again to war he pretends that he is to be married. Yet his fainthearted fear fools no one. After bearing much abuse, he explains himself to Leontes:

Leon: That in the midst of thy most hellish pains,
   When thou wert crawling-sick, didst aim at wonders?
   When thou wert mad with pain?
Lieut: Ye have found the cause out;
   I had ne'er been mad to fight else: I confess,
    sir,
   The daily torture of my side, that vex'd me,
   Make me as daily careless what became of me,
   Till a kind sword there wounded me, and eased me;
   'Twas nothing in my valour fought. I am well now,
   And take some pleasure in my life: methinks, now,
   It shew'd as mad a thing to me to see you scuffle,
   And kill one another foolishly for honour,
   As 'twas to you to see me play the coxcomb. (II, iv)

Not all the incidents are similar. For instance, the Lieutenant is temporarily deluded into believing he is ill again, thus causing a resurgence in his will to fight. Nevertheless, there are enough close resemblances here for one to feel sure of a decided influence.

In an earlier romantic drama by both Beaumont and Fletcher, *A King and no King,* comic relief is supplied by Bessus, a cowardly Captain, who will remind the reader of the Volunteers, Ariotto and Lizaro. His policy is to tell the truth, and the truth to him is always a splendid account of his own valor in the fray. More likely, however, Davenant was influenced in his depiction of these two vainglorious volunteers by Shakespeare.[9]

Falstaff and his ribald companions are always in our mind for in them, too, is pictured cowardice of a comical nature, cloaked and disguised in a boasting rant and bullying swagger. At the siege of Pisa, Ariotto and Lizaro are the first to cry "A battery! a battery!" (IV, 372) though they would be the last to venture into such a dangerous enterprise. In this they resemble Nym, Bardolph, and Pistol at the siege of Harfleur in *Henry V*:

Bard: On, on, on, on, on! to the breach, to the breach!
Nym: Pray thee, corporal, stay: the knocks are too hot; (III, ii)

---

[9] J. D. E. Williams, *Sir William Davenant's Relation to Shakespeare,* dissertation (Strassburg, 1905), p. 20 *passim.*

Just as Ariotto and Lizaro boast of their ability to hold Mervole
at bay, yet retreat ingloriously at his appearance, so does Falstaff
fail to observe his former threat to cudgel Prince Henry when the
Prince arrives. Note the following examples from Davenant:

Ario: ... Dost know Mervole?
Sora: You mean, Ensign Mervole, the duellist.
Ario: No matter for his title: we call each
      Other by the corruption of our names,
      Tom and Dick: 'Tis a blunt garb, but it
      Becomes soldiers. The slave is famous in
      Duels, he has proffered at us too; but
      We keep him at distance with a certain reverse.
      Observe me, sir! with a *punto sublimato*
      That is raised by your nether guard! present
      Your weapon naked!
             Enter Mervole, Piracco.
Liza: 'Slight! Here they are! End your discourse.
Ario: I shall attend you at your tent.
Sora: These are rare blades!   (IV, 376-377)

On the other hand, in *Henry IV, Part One*, we read:

Fals: How! the prince is a Jack, a sneak-cup: 'sblood, and he were
      here, I would cudgel him like a dog, if he would say so
            Enter the Prince etc. ...
Host: Nay, my lord, he called you Jack, and said he would cudgel
      you.
Fals: Did I, Bardolph?
Bard: Indeed, Sir John, you said so.
Fals: Yea, if he said my ring was copper.
Prin: I say 'tis copper: darest thou be as good as thy word now.
Fals: Why Hal, thou knowest, as thou art but man, I dare: but as
      thou art prince, I fear thee as I fear the roaring of the lion's
      welp. (III, iii)

Borrowing is more evident, however, in the account of the imagi-
nary battle that Ariotto and Lizaro fought with a band of Switzers.
In *Henry IV, Part One*, a masked Prince Henry and Poins frighten
Falstaff and his three companions into a ignominious flight. Later
they hear a most thrilling account that quite belies the truth.
Lizaro and Ariotto boast thus:

Liza: Ariotto, the maiden-head of this flesh
Is thine; this day thou didst deserve it by
Feats of valour.

Ario: Had I not seen thee engag'd against the
Other five, I had maintain'd the combat still
With those seven Switzers, – pox o'their two handed
Scythes! – it were easier for 'em to cut down
An oak than me, whilst I stood at this guard.

Liza: Right! but 'twas for the safety of my fame
To see you skirmish with twelve such,
And not employ my fortitude to weaken
Their assault. Can you accuse my fury?
For I beseech you, let us borrow your
Moderation.   (IV, 383)

For comparison, Falstaff's narration begins as follows:

Fals: Nay, that's past praying for, I have peppered two of them
– two I am sure I have paid, two rogues in buckram suits.
I tell thee what, Hal, if I tell thee a lie, spit in my face, call
me horse. Thou knowest my old ward. Here I lay, and thus
I bore my point. Four rogues in buckram let drive at me –

Prin: What, four? Thou saidst but two even now.

Fals: Four, Hal, I told thee four.

Poins: Aye, aye, he said four.

Fals: These four came all afront, and mainly thrust at me. I made
no more ado, but took all their seven points in my target, thus.

Prin: *Seven?* Why, there were but four even now. (II, iv)

As a whole *The Siege* owes nothing to Shakespeare, but in these
few characterizations, imitations are too marked to be ignored.

The one comic scene in the play which certainly is Davenant's
own in conception, containing some of that local color in which he
excels, was so appreciated by James Shirley that he thought nothing of appropriating it without a qualm. In *The Young Admiral*,
licensed July, 1633, and based mainly on a Spanish source, Shirley has inserted a dialogue between Pazzarello and a Sergeant that
is allied closely to a conversation between the Town Perdue and
Sergeant in *The Siege*: [10]

[10] Forsythe, *The Relationship of Shakespeare's Plays to Elizabethan
Drama* (New York, 1914), p. 197.

Serg: Follow me close; I hope you have made your will.

Pazz: My will? why, sergeant, I am not sick.

Serg: For all that you may be a dead man ere morning, – whiz!
(Firing heard)

Pazz: What's that?

Serg: These bullets will keep you waking! here, lie down close;
within two hours you shall be relieved.

Pazz: Dost hear, sergeant? (again) – whiz! do the enemies shoot
any sugar plums?

Serg: Be not too loud in your mirth; I see another give fire; farewell, signior Perdu.   (Exit)

Pazz: So, now I am a perdu! this will be news when I come home
again, the poor fellows will fall down and worship me. I always wonder'd why we had so many brave soldiers, and
quarrelling spirits; if they be shot-free, I cannot blame 'em to
roar so much in taverns – whiz! – again, I would fain have
one of these bullets hit me, that I might know certainly the
toughness of my new constitution, and yet I shall hardly be
sensible of it. In my conscience, if I were cramm'd into a
cannon, and shot into the town, like a cat I should light upon
my legs, and run home again.   (Lies down) (IV, iv)

In the Davenant drama, a like conversation reads:

Perd: Softly, Sergeant! we'd better walk on thorns than near the
enemy's perdues.

Serg: Follow still!

Perd: 'Sdeath! whither wilt thou lead me? shall we creep into their
cannons? We are already under their trenches.

Serg: Here, good Monsieur Perdue! lye down and dig a hole for
your chin.

Perd: Whize, hey! These bullets keep a noise; I shall not sleep for
'em.

Serg: Lye close! Within two hours you are relieved.

Perd: Dost hear, Sergeant? Fetch a notary from the town, and I'll
make my will, I bequeath thee my knap-sack; there's a hole
in the north side of't, sew it up! t'will prevent an invasion of
mice.

Serg: Y'are too loud in your mirth. I see a gun fire from the
redoubts.

Perd: Whize! Sergeant –

Serg: S'death! Speak low

Perd: I'n th' corner a' my ammunition cheese dwells a huge over-
grown maggot. I bequeath that to my comrade.

Serg: There's another gives fire. (*Exit*)
Perd: Whize! Farewell, good Sergeant! He's an old soldier. He knows the enemies shoot no sugar plums. (IV, 392-393)

It is noticed that both Pazzarello and the Town Perdue are to stand guard for two hours, and both refer to the bullet's noise and imitate its whistle. The making of their wills is mentioned in both plays, and in each the bullets are compared to sugar plums. The repetition of the word "perdu" and the designation of Davenant's character also helps to illustrate the indebtedness. It is truly surprising that Shirley should have appropriated such details so boldly and so soon after *The Siege* first appeared; in fact the belief that *The Siege* was not successful box office might be supported by Shirley's obvious theft. Years later in *The Imposture,* Shirley has a character named Bertoldi who accounts for his bravery in battle while being an abject coward, an episode which may or may not be influenced by Davenant's drama. As for *The Young Admiral,* there is no doubt.

Of these early subplots this is the most fully developed, occupying half the extant version of the play. And certainly it is the most comical. The satire here on gentlemen volunteers has none of the bitterness that is characteristic of his previous work. It is more concerned with the whimsical than the malicious. The braggadocio is like that of small boys. Ariotto proudly asserts that he never bothers with Ensign Mervole's title: "We call each / Other by the corruption of our names, Tom and Dick" (IV, 376). The hyperbolic flourishes of their boastings sound like the imaginative spoutings of a schoolboy:

Ario: The colonels and officers o'th' field
Avoid him with like haste, as they would –
Chain-shot.
Sora: Why, good signior?
Ario: They are eclipsed with his presence, as lesser
Lights before the sun: his valour drowns the voice
Of Hannibal and Scipio, he hath
Increased the number of the worthies, his name
Makes 'em up ten; you may see it i'th' last
Impression. (IV, 375)

And who can forget the sad lament that caps an hilarious display of craven fear: "Every man gains by quarreling, but we" (IV, 399). It is the right climax to their sorrows, immediately preceding the rise in their fortunes. For with the extraordinary *volte-face* in Piracco, they finally achieve the heretofore impossible. Almost as much as we enjoy the satisfaction of seeing a bully being bullied do we enjoy the amusing spectacle of these two weaklings luxuriating in an ardor of valor they never really knew before. Through all the farcical situations involving these irregular humorists, Davenant is more interested in poking fun than in being deliberately critical, and so he evokes a more genuine and prolonged laughter.

Once more it must be admitted that the intermingling of the two genres is not very skillful. By having Soranzo take part in both plots it is evident that Davenant has hoped to gain a greater singleness of impression. And the fact that the locale of both is the military is a decided asset in its favor. In any case, the flaw lies in the very success of the subplot. Always lively, colorful, and forcefully masculine, it dominates the effeminate major theme. The result is a swaggering comedy that drags in tow a central episode of seriously romantic sentiment that never artistically belongs.

THE JUST ITALIAN

In the above three plays it should be noticed that the comic conflict was largely among men. Although tragedies often depend almost entirely on heroes alone, it is less frequent, however, that comedies are purely masculine. The battle of the sexes is basic to life, and the laughter it generates is apparently one of the most primitive emotions. In his next tragicomedy Davenant adheres to the commoner conception of comedy as being bisexual and portrays for the first time this amusing antagonism. *The Just Italian,* licensed for the stage on October 2, 1629,[11] and later presented at Blackfriars, was, if we infer correctly from the words of Thomas

---

[11]   Harbage, p. 202.

Carew, not well received.[12] Nor was this salty comedy revived in the Restoration. Nevertheless, it contains some very good comedy, most worthy of discussion, and certainly suggestive of the excellences to be found in his yet-to-be written original comedies.

In the main plot Altamont, who has married a wealthy but untractable woman, Alteza, has determined to yoke her arrogant will. Parading Scoperta, his sister, about as his mistress, he hopes to stir his spouse's jealousy. Instead, she parries his blow by supposedly hiring the services of one Sciolto, one of the most obviously erotic young men in all drama. Since the emotions of both catspaws are never really tapped by their employers, it is not surprising that they turn to each other and fall in love. Altamont, misconstruing their true love for lust, cruelly censures his sister, then upbraids his wife, who, unknown to him, has just been reformed by the cruel taunts of a now virtuous Sciolto. At this point the plot becomes darkly complex with false tales of death, masked and muted mysterious guards, and violent quarrels. Luckily, imminent bloodshed stirs them all to display their essential integrity, and thus Altamont is convinced of his errors in judgment. With disaster averted, all ends happily.

The theme of a proud wife being tamed by a husband had pleased playwrights before Davenant, and it was to continue pleasing them later. The most famous example of it is, of course, Shakespeare's *The Taming of the Shrew*. Other versions which

---

[12]   Davenant, I, 206.

> These are the men in crowded heaps that throng
> To that adulterate stage, where not a tongue
> Of th' untun'd Kennel can a line repeat
> Of serious sense: but, like lips meet like meat;
> Whilst the true brood of Actors, that alone
> Keep natural unstrain'd action in her throne,
> Behold their benches bare, though they rehearse
> The terser Beaumont's or great Johnson's verse.
> Repine not thou then, since this churlish fate
> Rules not the stage alone; perhaps the State
> Hath felt this rancour, where men great and good
> Have by the rabble been misunderstood.
> So was thy Play, whose clear, yet lofty strain,
> Wisemen, that govern Fate, shall entertain.
> > Tho. Carew

would be equally familiar to an early seventeenth-century playwright were by Dekker and Fletcher. In the former's powerful
domestic drama, *The Honest Whore*, both parts have resemblances. In Part One, written very early in the century (1604), in
the comic subplot, Viola, Candido's wife, has her brother Fustigo
masquerade as her lover in order to vex her insufferably patient
husband. Like Sciolto, this lover swaggers and struts, but as far as
Candido is concerned, the ruse fails. The differences here are that
it is the wife who wishes to make the spouse jealous, not the husband, and that the plan fails entirely, unlike that of Altamont
which is successful to the extent that it provokes Alteza to counter
the insult. Part Two of *The Honest Whore,* produced a year later
than *The Just Italian*, in 1630, is actually closer in plot, for in this
part Candido takes for a second wife a rebellious woman who
requires his chastisement. And this she gets. Some twenty years
later than Part One of Dekker's drama, in Fletcher's rollicking
comedy *Rule a Wife and Have a Wife* (1624), the main plot details the trials of lusty Lady Margareta in her desire for a docile
husband. But in her marriage to Leon she is duped, for following
the ceremony he proves to be most domineering. Finally she
capitulates to him, throughly in love. Like Alteza, Lady Margareta
is also wealthy, and she too has no idea of marrying a dictatorial
male. All that which occurs in the steps towards the marriage in
this play by Fletcher, we might assume as having occurred before
the action takes place in *The Just Italian.*

Five years after Davenant failed with this play, Shirley appeared with *The Lady of Pleasure,* perhaps his finest comedy. In this
we watch the spectacle of a willful wife, who allows herself more
license than Alteza, being brought to repentance by the artful
contrivances of her husband. Lady Bornwell, like Alteza, is fond
of reminding her spouse of their different social backgrounds,
evidently assuming that her noble ancestry justifies her desire for
marital independence. Thus she embarks on an escapade with
Littleworth. Bornwell, more even-tempered than Altamont, an-
nounces that he will outdo his wife in revelry, and proceeds to do
so without seeming unduly worried over her immoral actions. Part
of his plan is to introduce one Celestina as his mistress. Eventually

Lady Bornwell is cowed, and her conversion can be parelleled to that of Alteza, incidentally a reformation that points towards that of a direct literary descendant, Sheridan's Lady Teazle. One remarkable distinction between these two plays, though they are only five years apart, is that the Shirley play is not nearly so vicious in dialogue or so depraved in lustful action as the former. Shirley's atmosphere is closer to that of the Restoration mode, is more foppish, light and graceful, without any of Davenant's obvious crudities in style and spirit.

Marital strife, when human emotions are not too closely involved, is a comic display, because it is contrary to the ideal union which the intellect asserts is desirable. Two human beings who are basically in harmony but who refuse to agree because of sharply defined egos produce a most incongruous picture. But if emotion enters into the situation, the comedy departs. Such an example is the Altamont-Alteza quarrel in *The Just Italian*. Each is enough attracted to the other to wish to assert the major role in the union. Each is equally unwilling to submit to the other. There is no emotion to this disharmony; it is purely a matter of human wills. Thus it is not long before the spectator recognizes that the comedy present is pointing towards the Restoration comedy of manners. Here we have two strong-willed personalities dealing with an essentially social problem. It contains a cuckold theme that was always good for laughter in the Restoration age, and it is displayed with a modicum of wit. Alteza represents the "new woman", prototype of the Restoration woman of wit who wanted her independence recognized. Altamont expresses her type thus:

> Her crime to spring, not from poison'd malice
> But, from the feminine mistakes of wit:
> For, modern courts now preach, wit doth reside
> In ladies' subtle riots, and their pride.   (I, 210)

Sometime later, following considerable concern for his marital plight, he assails her harshly for her gravest crime: "Thou wouldst usurp the charter of the male" (I, 214). Such extensive analysis of his wife leaves no doubt about his feeling for his wife. He wants her, to be sure, yet he wants her to want him as her master. On the other hand, she, already spoiled by wealth and position, suffers from delusions of her own importance. Nor has she any clear idea of what her goal should be. In rejecting the traditional role as lady of the house, she does not quite know what role will replace it. Thus when she does express an aim, it is done necessarily with intentional absurdity, as in her haughty demand that her orchard be paved with agates. Emancipated without understanding why, Alteza suggests here the bargaining scenes so skillfully depicted in Restoration comedy, and in doing so she is ridiculous enough to be highly diverting.

With the introduction of the Sciolto-Scoperta episode, the situations become too bemired for good taste. Altamont describes too lushly Scoperta's kisses, and Alteza boasts much too wantonly of her "stallion". Fortunately for them, the spectator knows that their infidelities are faked, incidentally a situation opposite to the usual Restoration treatment. Thus the comic irony of the situation allows us to laugh more freely, for we know that neither character is quite so morally lax as each pretends to the spouse. At times Sciolto's proud claims for his astonishing sexual prowess might be unsettling, but these moments are usually compensated for by the spectacle of an Altamont who is quite unable to taste his own medicine. Here is the double-standard motif always common to the male-female relationship, and therefore always thoroughly comic. At this point Altamont deserves such unkind treatment from his wife, and thus he precludes all our sympathy. In fact, all is still mirthful until Sciolto, in order to avoid the obvious advances of Alteza, scornfully rebukes her. Though we understand the reasons for his actions, we never feel that they are quite justified. Nevertheless, this ungallant behavior on his part does have the salutary effect of reforming the errant wife. From here on the comedy element diminishes rapidly, even though the several disguises reflect certain conventions common to comedy of intrigue. Alteza no longer thinks, but feels. It is the same with Altamont. Emotions become rife, and the situation is darkly colored with tragic overtones. This plot never again regains its comic aspect. What began as a fairly deft comedy of manners moves through some unnecessary crudities into an emotional debauch of sentimental pathos. It is impossible to forgive Davenant for such an excrescence in the use of dramatic tone.

The subplot of *The Just Italian* is more consistently treated. In this Florello, the impecunious but enterprising brother of Alta-mont, arrives back from the wars with an earnest wish to marry well. Despite his brother's marital discord, he determines to woo the rich sister of Alteza. With a substantial loan from Altamont, he is able to make a magnificent impression upon the eligible Charintha. As might be expected, since he is masquerading as Dandolo, a rich Milanese count, the real Dandolo arrives. The problem then is which one is going to prove the other an impostor. After much hilarious raillery Florello's identity is eventually dis-covered, but it is no matter to regret, for the romantic girl has already fallen in love. Without any qualms for the future, Charin-tha fondly offers herself to the bogus suitor.

Fortune-hunting is a theme in drama much too prevalent to be analyzed here with any value. In the seventeenth century, for in-stance, there are several plays with a plot element similar to this. Shirley's *The Sisters* is an example which appeared over ten years after Davenant's work. It has a story of a robber, named Frapolo, who disguises himself as the Prince of Parma, with his banditti as his suite, in order to court and marry the rich Paulina. The irony inherent in such a plot will probably always win an audience. But the one play that most closely resembles this underplot is Van-brugh's *The Relapse*. In this Restoration comedy the insolvent younger brother, Young Fashion, courts a wealthy country girl under the guise of his brother Lord Foppington, in a manner very similar to the deception perpetrated in *The Just Italian*. Likewise the rightful figure turns up to claim his own, but in the end fails in his quest, for the impostor has already won the heart of the girl. The general tenor of the two plots is so alike that it is not easy to deny any influence.

The comic element that is most evident in this underplot is gen-erally well sustained. Except for the sentimental ending, much of it is of the comic variety that would be expected of two emanci-pated sisters being rapidly hoodwinked by the very brother of the man they protest to deplore. Nevertheless, were the impostor and the Count he impersonates less richly conceived, the episode would lack much of its spice. Perhaps no scene quite equals in fund of humor that in which Florello first arrives as Charintha's Milanese suitor. Extravagantly generous he disposes rare jewels with a careless "I have enow. Wear 'em" (I, 230). Charmingly churlish, he answers Alteza's eager requests to be noticed by requesting his servant to remember her for him. His mode of life is unusually bizarre:

> I've instruments distinct, that take a charge
> O'th'several quarters of my frame, my dwarf
> Doth dress me up unto the knees, and, when
> His stature leaves his reach, young Virgins then,
> Th'issue of decay'd barons, do begin
> And govern to the navel. Whilst upwards,
> Barbers, painters, and parasites are us'd. (I, 231)

It is no wonder that the real Count will have difficulty in combatting such a flamboyant gentleman. Yet in quite a different way he is almost a better comic creation. Less farcical and more a "humor" in concept, he realizes his own inability to compete on the same level with his beguiling impersonator. Though thoroughly insulted by Florello and not warmly received by the two ladies, he is by principle too calm to expostulate hotly. Violence, he prefers to settle verbally when possible; when utterly necessary he enlists the services of his two bravos, Staccato and Punto, two Jonsonian humors, whose discreet ferocity is delightfully absurd. Admittedly he is a conceited prig, yet an ingratiating one. Nevertheless, we are pleased that a genial rogue has bettered him in love's pursuit.

The high quality of comedy in these scenes and characters is amplified by the sprightly dialogue. Witty and alert, it keeps the episodes moving with a briskness that is quite necessary if one is to overlook a very serious fault in poorly motivated characterization. For example, in the main plot it is quite unlikely that Alteza would reform so rapidly. Nor are we prepared for the surprise of Sciolto's startling conversation. Only outrageous pandering to the public appetite for sentiment can explain such weakness in character delineation. Even those who will not forgive this major flaw, however, will admit that *The Just Italian,* as a transitional comedy, containing humors and intrigue aspects while moving in the manners direction, is replete with some extremely funny comedy. One would readily believe that Davenant is now ready to write *The Wits*, his first original comedy.

LOVE AND HONOUR

Following his success with *The Wits*, Davenant did not disappoint his admirers. *Love and Honour* was to become his most popular and most influential tragicomedy. Its title alone was to make theatre history as the official designation of a particular dramatic genre. Though it was originally titled *The Courage of Love,* and later retitled *The Nonpareilles; or, The Matchless Maids*, the final title boded more for Davenant's importance since it was a bold announcement that he was courting the favor of the Queen. Henrietta Maria, having long been interested in the Platonic cult she had been exposed to in France, thought the time propitious to make it heard at the English court. Successful dramatic versions of a love-and-honor theme would immeasurably boost her cause. And the dramatist who could do it for her would immeasurably boost his own cause.

This success Davenant enjoyed. So applauded was it that the queen refused to let it die. During the plague, in the winter of 1636-37, when theatres were closed, she had it revived at Hampton Court. Soon after Charles II restored the monarchy he bestowed upon it the rare honor of having presented a production that was outfitted in his own coronation robes. Pepys was so impressed that he paid it a second visit, calling it "a very good play".[13] For years it held the stage as one of the staples of the Duke's company, and as late as 1720 a three-act comedy by Charles Molloy, "The Half-pay Officers", was influenced by its farcical underplot.[14] For the second time Davenant pleased his public, but for the first time he predicted what the public would continue to find pleasing.

[13] Pepys' entry for October 23, 1661.
[14] Davenant, III, 94.

The plot is much too intricate to detail closely, nor would it be necessary for our discussion of comedy. In an Italian war Evandra, the daughter of the Duke of Milan, is captured by the forces of the Duke of Savoy. Loved by the latter's son, Alvaro, she is safely concealed from the Duke's desire for blood revenge of an old crime. Concealed with her in the house of Prospero, a young Count who also loves her, is Melora, sister of Leonell, her third suitor. Determined that the fair charmer will not be executed, each of the three heroes vies for the honor of the supreme sacrifice. Equally determined is Evandra that only she will suffer. Melora, too, seems eager for self-immolation and palms herself off as Evandra so as to be executed in her place. Following a bewildering display of heroic attitudes and doffed disguises, it is surprisingly revealed that the old Duke of Savoy had believed in a crime that never really existed. Revenge being unnecessary, amity is restored all round, and the rewards of true love and true honor are displayed with happy sentiment. Complex as this plot is to us today, annoyingly so in fact, in its own time it would have pleased. According to Alfred Harbage, Caroline audiences loved a "puzzle interest",[15] that is the kind of plot which kept the spectator continually curious until the last startling surprise. And when the plot could express all their favorite sentiments with a certain nobility of language, so much the better. Davenant has wisely gauged his audience.

With the upswing of interest in sentiment, the role of comedy in drama began to diminish. Still, in a concentrated dose, its impact could even be stronger. Such is the case here. The farcical underplot exploiting the popular fortune-hunting theme is fully developed within a somewhat shorter time space than Davenant had heretofore used in tragicomedy. In it Colonel Vasco, a comically coarse soldier, woos and wins an old wealthy widow of one hundred and ten years. His hopes of soon inheriting her dowry are promptly blasted when her several infirmities prove to be of no great seriousness. Regretting his haste, he craves a divorce, and after more than a few anxious moments the Duke comes to his aid.

[15]   Harbage, p. 231.

As we noticed in discussing the underplot of *The Just Italian* fortune-hunting was a theme already used too widely for one to discuss direct influences. Davenant would be aware of many of them, such as one that has already been noted as a possible influence, Fletcher's comic masterpiece *Rule a Wife and Have a Wife*. In this the underplot of Perez-Estifania, derived from Cervantes, concerns a fortune-hunter Michael Perez, who is gulled in his marriage to Estifania for she does not possess the great wealth she has boasted. In time, too, they reconcile. Thus we see that the resemblance is really rather thin as it is in all such plays containing this theme. Davenant, more experienced and with a success behind him, could rely now more heavily on his own inventiveness. Thus in developing a situation that must have been the subject of more than one bawdy joke during his army days, of copulation with an old crone, he may have been at times obnoxiously crude, but he was wonderfully comic.

Four scenes in particular are particularly lively. In the first he is planning his strategy upon the woman he has already described quite unfavorably:

> ... and yet, forsooth,
> His prisoner must be fair, and young, and mine
> So old she might have given Hercules suck;
> Now she sucks too, for she hath no teeth left.
> In one month she'll cost me as much in caudles
> And sweet candy as her ransom comes to. (III, 102-103)

In voicing his aims to his cronies, Vasco honestly appraises his intentions and his expected rewards. The Widow is deaf, and so he will not have to woo with music; she has no teeth, and so requires no banquets; and she is "no more fit for the business of encrease / Than I am to be a nun" (III, 128). But the sacrifice is worth it, for he plans with his newly acquired wealth to cut a very splendid figure indeed. Davenant has certainly whetted his spectator's appetite to see the woman in question.

When the Widow does appear, she is all that has been promised. And on this occasion her deafness provides the comedy. Vasco and his comrades boldly insult her in terms which her maid relates to her in the most flattering manner. Not a shred of kindness is present in the taunts she never hears. And yet there is little cruelty felt in their stinging jibes, for the old wretch is too silly to be sympathetic. When she accepts the proposal of a man young enough to be her grandson, she forfeits our serious consideration. Nevertheless, her command to her maid in preparation for the wedding ceremony stirs our amused curiosity for Vasco's promised bliss:

> Lelia, provide a broom
> And sweep away the rheum near the green couch:
> And, d'you hear, look for one of my cheek teeth
> Which dropt under the wainscot-bed.   (III, 142)

Vasco's expected fate materializes as we hoped, for he too deserves all that he receives. Following a bawdy serenade offered by his friends, he appears on stage to groan about his marital blessings. Nor can his friends resist teasing him. In his words, "I'm risen from the dead, from bones more dusty / Than theirs, that did begin their sleep beneath / A marble coverlet, some thousand years ago" (III, 156-157). Worse still is the fact that his new wife seems to grow fonder of his person. Her death, he desperately expects, will be imminent, for she ails so extravagantly. Still she cautions him not to worry because "'Tis but a fit that ever takes me once / In fifty years: but weep not! 'twill away" (III, 158). Is is not surprising that in the fourth scene, when the Widow is anxiously hurrying to witness an execution, the weary Vasco weakly hopes that she will be crushed in the crowds or flattened under a hastily-built scaffold. Yet none of these statements is nearly so grisly as it sounds, for none of the characters is any more than superficially pictured, and always in absurdly improbable situations. We laugh because it is all too ludicrous to be real.

Given such a plot and such characters with an army background, it is no problem to forgive the ribaldry that abounds in the dialogue. Soldiers' talk is smutty, and smutty Davenant makes it. But it suits the situation. When Vasco speaks against female executions because a woman without a head cannot kiss properly, we laugh in shocked surprise, but in retrospect we realize that a blunt soldier is capable of such a jest. Davenant knew his soldiers well. He also had a real flare for dramatizing local color. By taking the earthy color of army life he was able to present an essentially bawdy subplot in such a manner that it rarely, except to the prudish, would offend. Better still, by having a military background for two plots that are well motivated, though artificial, he did his best job to date of providing a unity of effect. The comic relief has been adroitly spaced among some mawkish sentiments so that it not only diverts the attention with laughter but also serves to emphasize in contrast the inherent nobility of mind present in the leading characters. Singleness of impression in tragicomedy, he finally achieved.

THE PLATONICK LOVERS

The rewards of dramatizing the love and honor theme being solidly proved, Davenant pursued it again in *The Platonick Lovers*, licensed on November 16, 1635.[16] Being concerned almost consistently with a topical subject, it had the fate of most topical plays. The novelty soon died, and there is no record of its revival. Then, too, the semi-serious tone adopted in the play may well have hampered its possibilities of lasting longer. Neither supporting the Platonic theory entirely, probably because he himself found it unsympathetic, nor ridiculing it completely because of the Queen's sentimental attitude, Davenant equivocates throughout and thus weakens its dramatic force. However, there is enough comedy present to make clear that if Davenant had treated it entirely as a farce, he would have written a wonderfully funny play.

Theander and Phylomont, two ruling Dukes, are each in love with the other's sister, the former with Eurithea, and the latter with Ariola. But their love differs. Whereas Phylomont is so unholy as to love with physical desire, Theander's passion is completely mental. He has etherealized the emotion to a state of unreal ideality. A fifth person present at the court, one Fredeline, who secretly lusts for Eurithea, resolves to complicate matters to his own satisfaction. Thus he enlists the services of a known

[16] Sir Henry Herbert, *The Dramatic Records of Sir Henry Herbert* (New Haven, 1917), p. 37.

physician, Buonateste, who reputedly possesses a potent love elixir, such as existed in Shakespeare's *A Midummer Night's Dream* or in Fletcher's *The Humorous Lieutenant.* Meanwhile the two Dukes have become estranged by Phylomont's request for Ariola as a wife. The horrified Theander upbraids his sister for being so "unnatural" and locks her in seclusion. Soon he is to regret his accusations, for when the potion begins to work, he is overpowered by a seemingly uncontrollable sexual desire. It is necessary for Eurithea to veil herself to ensure protection of her virtue. Naturally Theander apologizes to his former friend and permits a marriage, and then he himself successfully proposes. To Phylomont's chagrin, however, his Ariola has been convinced of the Platonic view and now deems marriage undesirable. Eurithea does marry though and is radiantly happy until it is suggested that she bed with her spouse. In great shame for his "crime" Theander bids her adieu and leaves in sorrow, vowing never to see her again. At this point the plot becomes quite complex. The unscrupulous Fredeline, aided by some guileless servants, presses his attack, until he overplays too vigorously his hand. Poisoned by Buonateste he becomes an "unfortunate Platonic gentleman", just as the two ladies, noting their folly, return to their Dukes to live in natural wedded harmony.

Unwilling to affront the ladies of the court who fondly affirmed this unfruitful theory, Davenant does make an attempt to present Theander and Ariola in a favorable light. And basically his treatment of them is serious, for this is not a light comedy of manners. It is a modern social problem that he knows he should treat with some sobriety. Without his heart in it, however, he fails to conceal his own amused contempt. When Theander denounces Phylomont for wanting to espouse Eurithea, his most forceful rebuke is "You are too masculine" (II, 48). This primness in a man of his calibre is not flattering. His excrutiating agony in subjecting a woman to marriage is difficult to accept with a sober countenance:

> O cruel stars!
> I shall betray a virgin now, whose innocence
> Is so extreme it yields, and turns to guilt. (II, 71)

Surely if Davenant wanted his audience to accept the theory, he would have avoided such melodramatic speeches in his hero!

Other characters help to make this Platonic doctrine appear silly. Sciolto, a friendly old lord, is sensibly dubious:

> Right, sir, for I believe those babies he
> And Eurithea do beget by gazing in
> Each other's eyes, can inherit nothing, –
> I mean by th' custom here in Sicily.
> As for Plato's love-laws they may entail
> Lands on ghosts and shadows, for aught I know:
> I understand not Greek.   (II, 20)

Added to this is the comic disdain of wise Buonateste, who refused to allow Plato to be blamed for such rank stupidity:

Scio: Unto no other but my son: I find
He's very much platonically given.
Buon: My Lord, I still beseech you not to wrong
My good friend Plato, with this Court calumny;
They father on him a fantastic love
He never knew, poor gentleman. Upon
My knowledge, sir, about two thousand years
Ago, in the high street yonder
At Athens, just by the corner as you pass
To Diana's conduit, – a haberdasher's house,
It was, I think, – he kept a wench!
Scio: How, sir, a wench!
Buon: I could say more; my friend was lewdly given.
Scio: But with your favour, sir, a plump brown wench?
Buon: Faith, authors differ about that; some write
She had a flaxen hair, and others too,
That did not blush to know more private marks,
Say she had a mole under her left thigh
Others a hollow tooth, that put him to
The charge of cloves, because her breath
Grew somewhat troublesome.
Fred: Give me thy hand,
Doctor; I'll have some share too in thy heart
Ere long. But did not Plato write of love?
Buon: Divinely, sir. But not such kind of love
As ladies would have now: they mistake him. (II, 38-39)

Plato may be coarsely defamed here, but in any case Buonateste has made his own attitude clear. On the other hand the villainous

Fredeline despises Platonic love, too, which may speak in its favor were we not to notice why he is so scornful:

Cast: My sister, signior, is inquisitive,
Guilty of my offence, she ask'd me ere
You came, why you endeavour'd thus to have
The lady married to another, whom you meant to love?
Fred: That's the platonic way; for so
The balls, the banquets, chariot, canopy,
And quilted couch, which are the places where
This new wise sect do meditate, are kept,
Not at the lover's but the husband's charge.
And it is fit; for marriage makes him none,
Though she be still of the society.
Amad: And may, besides her husband, have
A sad platonical servant to help her meditate.
Fred: All modern best court authors do allow't.
Amad: You give good light into the business, sir. (II, 52)

In such dialogue as this it is all too evident that this innocent theory could be so easily, and probably was, propounded for nefarious motives. It is surely ironic justice that at the conclusion the arch-plotter should bewail that quite against his own inclination, he has been made an "unfit Platonic gentleman". As if this were not injury enough, Phylomont adds the crowning insult to the noble doctrine:

Whining and puling love is fit for eunuchs,
And for old revolted nuns.   (II, 104)

In addition to this not too veiled satire of individuals who, like some of Shakespeare's comic characters, have veered from a plane of common sense and have to be ridiculed back to order again, Davenant has poked some fun at the expense of the intellectuals. In Act Three when Sciolto and Fredeline doubt the efficacy of Buonateste's potion, they have some merry sport at the expense of not only his learning but that of all academicians and scientists:

Fred: Since your great Master Aristotle died,
Who fool'd the drunken Macedon out of
A thousand talents to buy books, what have

The multitude of's learn'd successors done?
Wrote comments on his works; 'light! I could beat
You all, Have you so many ages toil'd
T' interpret what he writ in a few years?
Is there yet nothing new, to render benefit
For human life, or strengthen reason for
Our after hopes? Why do we build you colleges?

Scio: Yes, and allow 'em pensions too, that they
May scribble for no end, but to make paper dear.

Buon: For one unlucky scape in knowledge must
I suffer all this tyranny?

Scio: You study physic too?

Fred: He knows to cure sick chickens o'th' pip.

Scio: I'ld fain see one of that profession live
Five hundred years without loss of a tooth.

Fred: No, sir. They'll suffer ruin and decay
In their own bodies for examples' sake,
That others may fall sick and make 'em rich.

Scio: Right, Fredeline, for notwithstanding all
Their min'rals and their herbs, we must be fain
At last to betake our selves to the wide yawn,
Grinning, and the long stretch.

Buon: You make all knowledge
But deception, sir; and cheaters of the learn'd philosophers.

Fred: 'Troth, little less. The merry fop of Thrace
That always laugh'd, pretending 'twas at vanity;
Alas, 'twas his disease! Going to steal
Mushrooms for his supper, the blue mouth'd serpent skulk'd
Under a dock leaf, and bit him by the thumb,
From whence he took that laughing malady.

Scio: And his antagonist would ever seem
To weep, out of a pious cause. A fine
Dissembling fellow: 'twas not sorrow made him weep.

Buon: No sir? make that appear.

Scio: I'll show a manuscript,
Now kept i' th' Vatican that proves
He had nine years a fistula in's eye.

Fred: Mere coz'ners all!

Scio: As for Diogenes, that fasted much
And took his habitation in a tub,
To make the world believe he lov'd a strict
And severe life, he took the diet, sir,
And in that very tub sweat for the French disease.

Fred: And some unlearn'd apothecary since,
Mistaking's name, called it Cornelius Tub.
Buon: My noble friends, make such still of your spleens,
Tickle your selves with straws, if you want sport;
I shall have my revenge ere long.   (II, 56-57)

This is not the first time that Davenant had jested about learned men and their methods. There have been snide remarks before. Other playwrights, too, had adopted a similar attitude. Marston in *What you Will* writes a speech for one Lampatho in which he derides the attitude of a "scholler" (II, i). Nevertheless, Davenant's satire is really quite jovial, for as the play progresses we note that not only is Buonateste's potion proved valid, but he gradually unveils himself as the most sensible, if skeptical, individual in the drama, a sort of Shakespearean commentator.

With such generous satire as is mentioned here, with the humor of the capricious ladies reversing their attitudes at inopportune moments, and abetted by a bawdy maid, Amadine, whose thoughts on marriage are in line with those of Juliet's nurse, Davenant has written for his main plot one that is often more comic than serious, depending greatly, of course, on one's attitude to the doctrine slyly being debunked. But nowhere is the humor quite so riotous as that which decorates the underplot.

Soon after the drama begins we learn through Sciolto's conversation that he momentarily expects a son he has not seen in thirteen years. Desiring to experiment, he had the boy sent to an army camp with firm instructions to the governor that the lad ". . . should never learn to write nor read, / Nor never see a woman" (II, 11). Believing that learning makes men conceited and women make them fools, it is his hope that freedom from both will enable a youth to mature into a finer specimen of humanity than is usual. Naturally the spectator eagerly anticipates the result, already knowing the fun to be gained from a similar situation in Shakespeare's *The Tempest*.

From his entrance Gridonell, the misplaced person in an established social pattern, is a humorous buffoon. Halfway between a Jonsonian "humor" and an Elizabethan fool, it is his part to crack the coarsest jokes and rouse the most marked and unsophisticated laughter, a kind of laughter that is heartier and healthier than that generated in the main plot and, therefore, a desirable contrast.

The first woman Gridonell is to encounter is Amadine, who is "old and poor" and, therefore, in the judgment of Sciolto, safe enough for sociability. She may be homely to the aging man, but to the hale son, who never saw a female, she is a rare sight. He is convinced that she is "an angel of the better sort: some lieutenant / Colonel in heaven . . ." (II, 25). The uneasy woman, impatient to prove the truth, rashly urges him to feel her warmth. When this proves of little help, she concludes that he is mad and hastens to leave. Throughout this episode the comedy is increased by the placement of Sciolto in the background as a shocked observer of his son's reactions. James Shirley liked this idea so much that he adopted it in *The Humorous Courtier*, written about five years later. In that play there is a scene with Comachio, commenting in stupefaction as he witnesses his nephew Depazzi, a foolish chap, pay court to a Duchess. Circumstances are altered, but the protestations of affection of two bumbling boys give rise to the same sort of surprise to their relatives.

In this scene one notes in particular how Gridonell praises his new love in army terminology. She has "the prettiest pinking eyes; / The holes are no bigger than a pistol bore". "Her fingers are so small, and longer than a drumstick" (II, 26). It is a device that Congreve will use in *Love for Love* in order to characterize Ben, a sailor, who has known women but has been kept from them so long that his hot desire is the equal of Gridonell's mania. The difference is, of course, that he favors a mariner's language to a soldier's. Even Gridonell's sparse army knowledge of French is to be used to aid the game of love. He is told that "Que va la" will serve when meeting a mistress in the dark, and that "Randee vous" could be used for an obstinate wench who is reluctant to yield. Then, too, his army knowledge of music, the use of drum and trumpet, is not to be scorned. With such an untutored figure to mock, the courtiers naturally have a field day, and in doing so the comic irony proves hilarious to an audience.

The broadest comedy is provided in Gridonell's last important appearance on stage. He, too, has been given Buonateste's elixir and is reacting as expected. His lust drives him into a frenzy. Still he is unaware of what his emotions are. When he begs for a woman he offers a baffling explanation:

> ... I've occasion to use her
> Something I must do, I know not what 'tis,
> But I begin to feel she will be very
> Convenient for me at this time. (II, 73)

Fortunately, he does have enough knowledge to refuse the offer of a six-month babe, and he is sure of his tastes to the extent that a "dead commodity" does not appeal. But he is not above requesting his father to pimp for him. Aghast at such unbridled behavior, Sciolto is convinced of his own folly. For the protection of all maidenheads, he has his son imprisoned until the fever passes. It is no surprise at the play's conclusion when Sciolto resolves to mend his mistakes in the erroneous tutelage of his son.

The robust comedy of this underplot is just right to complement the satirical element otherwise noted, especially when both plots are allied in being indirectly didactic. That is, Davenant is taking a frank attitude towards love and lust, removing the misconceptions and emphasizing the hard core of truth. With a clear mind he sees the ideal love as being compounded of both the physical and the spiritual, each serving to bolster the other. To deny one is to exaggerate the other, causing eventual tumult in the human situation. And to ensure this right-minded attitude, society must see that theories of training are, above all, sensible, never the result of fashion or whim. It was a capital idea for a comedy, and often Davenant succeeds. Had he cared less to please the court, his comedy might have been abhorred, but with his gifts it would surely have been a greater work.

THE UNFORTUNATE LOVERS

In 1638, following an interval of two years, which were plague years with the theatres seldom open, Davenant produced in rapid succession two plays, one tragedy titled *The Unfortunate Lovers* and a tragicomedy titled *The Fair Favourite*. The first was royally received at the time, and later in the Restoration it was one of the first plays to be revived. *The Fair Favourite*, licensed on November 17, 1638,[17] was presented before the Queen at the Cockpit, but, without records to prove it, it is doubtful if it enjoyed the reception his tragedy received earlier in the year.

The Unfortunate Lovers is a tragedy of blood, incorporating generous elements of the sentimental at which Davenant was so adept. Galeotto, a scheming court counsellor of the Prince of Verona, desiring the Duke Altophil for his own daughter, Amaranta, accuses the Duke's betrothed Arthiopa of unchastity. The Prince demotes his villainous counsellor when the ruse is exposed, and then suggests that the Duke marry Amaranta so that he himself may possess the fair Arthiopa. Throughout these sorry stratagems the virtuous Amaranta begins to shine as an ideal of her sex, and she continues to do so after the barbarian King Heildebrand of the Lombards enters to complicate matters. He, too, lusts after the hapless Arthiopa. The enraged Duke slays Galeotto, thereby causing Amaranta, in guilty grief for her father's death, to commit suicide. Heildebrand dies for his crime of raping Arthiopa, and immediately afterwards she and her Duke expire in each other's arms. In this bath of blood of the six leading characters, only the Prince remains alive.

Fortunately, Davenant does not allow the horrors of this Italianate tragedy to go unrelieved. At the beginning of the play appears one Rampino, a young gallant soldier, and his two companions, Brusco and Hirco. Like the typical crude army men he has pictured before, making the usual obscene remarks, they do not really provide any sure comedy until the second act. At this time enters Friskin, a tailor, looking for Rampino, who, like Witgood in Middleton's *A Trick to Catch the Old One,* is evidently a constant source of vexation to his creditors. In the brief exchange of dialogue we learn that Rampino has changed his quarters thrice in two days in order to avoid being contacted. Thus he is surprised when Friskin finds him. Still without money, this time he diverts the tailor from his pursuit by enquiring about the newest fashions. The next time they encounter in Act Three, Rampino's artifice is

17   Nethercot, p. 165.

even more skilled. He flatters his creditors into forgetting their objective. To the importunate Friskin he promises preferment as the king's tailor. Moreover, he promises to aid Friskin's brother, a shoemaker, as well. It is not long before Friskin, having forgotten his original goal, is eager to measure Rampino for a new suit of clothes. Likewise, to Fibbia, a precise widow to whom he is also indebted, he is equally artful. In addition to praising her youthful appearance, he hints of an available position as rocker to the yet unborn prince. Beguiled at the honorable prospect, she too is easily shaken from her previous quest. The idea here was sufficiently diverting to impress John Wilson for his *The Projectors*. In this later play Gotham pursues Jocose in payment of a debt, but Driver, Jocose's servant, puts him off by offering to let him in on a promising experiment. The parallel is obvious.

Such minor comedy as there is in this tragedy is discreetly manipulated so as not to impair the general tenor of the drama. Not only are the soldiers involved well integrated into the main plot, but their comic appearances are quite in keeping with their professional status. In fact, so tasteful is the comic relief that it was evidently too tame for Restoration audiences. In the 1673 folio edition, in addition to the interpolation of some songs, Friskin becomes excessively vulgar in his comments.[18] No psychological reason for such obscenity is apparent; it could only exist to titillate a jaded audience. Had Davenant left the comedy as he previously composed it, one would accept it as being very slight, indeed, yet serving unobtrusively as welcome comic relief in a gloomy tragedy.

THE FAIR FAVOURITE

The heroine of *The Fair Favourite* is the Platonic mistress of a married monarch. Though Eumena's relationship is without a physical aspect, still her presence causes several unsettling crises. Her brother Oramont, unwilling to believe in her innocence, denounces her violently and even reviles his former comrade Amadore for defending the girl. A duel is fought between them in

[18]   Davenant, III, 90.

which Amadore is supposedly slain. For this crime Oramont is condemned to die, an execution that is averted by the discovery of a very much alive Amadore. At the happy conclusion the King conceives a sudden affection for his long-suffering queen, thus offering Eumena the freedom to bestow herself on Amadore. As the nuptial rites are being prepared, Oramont claims that war will be his mistress until he can expiate his uncontrollable jealousy.

Into this diluted mixture of heroics and sentiment, Davenant has injected a small dose of court satire. It first occurs when a couple of gentlemen comment disdainfully on several Old Courtiers who enter stage chatting among themselves. "The living furniture o' th' Court", they take it ill that they are not rich for they have brainlessly tired themselves in the king's service, having "worn out his Grace's hangings with / Their backs, and, with their feet, his mats" (IV, 237). Their next appearance on stage is certainly more inauspicious, for they are described as "picking their teeth, and striking off crumbs from their skirts" (IV, 250). Though they never speak directly to the audience, but only appear ridiculous in pantomime, their female counterparts are quite vocal. One by one three such ladies arrive, each initially gracious to the others, then maliciously critical when beyond ear distance. Supporting this hypocrisy is a courtier who practises the same insincerity, lauding a lady to her person, then speaking ill of her bad breath to another.

Davenant's gift for picturing local color is extended here to the life at court. To judge by his satire, one would well infer that the dramatist's experiences with some of the inhabitants of the court had been none too pleasant. Surely his opinions of the lightness in which they contemplated executions was coldly cynical (IV, 265-266). Though such satire was common in Shakespeare before the time of the Jacobeans in which it abounds, one can well infer that Davenant is not directly influenced; he is probably working within a popular tradition in order to release some pent-up indignation. Moreover, it occupies a very minor part of his play, although it adroitly fixes a decadent atmosphere, thereby increasing the plausibility of the tragicomic tale it features. Thus here, as in *The Unfortunate Lovers,* Davenant wisely refrains from allowing his

comic elements to exceed their need, and so they never intrude to
violate the unity of impression. Instead, with the pleasure of variety, they help to complete it.

THE DISTRESSES

The last play written by Davenant before Parliament decided to
shut down all playhouses was *The Distresses*. Licensed in November, 1639, under the title of *The Spanish Lovers*, it was acted
then, though apparently never again.[19] The unending complexities
of the plot and the often inflated heroics of the dialogue probably
precluded any popular support. Nevertheless, there are comic features of the plot that are very worthy of consideration, particularly
those that foreshadow Restoration modes.

A detailed summary of the plot would in itself be so complex
that it would not have the happy effect of elucidating the many
intricacies of action. Therefore it will suffice to account briefly for
the major developments in plotting. Set in Cordova, Spain, the
serious portion of the play concerns Claramante, whose beauty
has caused her and others much discomfort. Her most intemperate
brother, Leonte, rashly resenting her desirability, is too irate to
even thank one of her suitors, Dorando, for having saved the life
of another brother, Balthazar. Later, hoping to intercept a moon-
light visit of this Dorando, he mistakes Orgemon, who, by chance,
is nearing Claramante's dwelling for the same romantic purpose,
and begins a duel. Leonte is thrown. Claramante entreats for his
life. Orgemon agrees, and for his kindness he is unjustly stabbed
by Leonte. Fortunately, he survives and is soon recovered, willing
to satisfy Claramante's request that he safely sequester her from
Leonte's wrath. Dressed as a man, she is led by Orgemon to the
house of his friend, a notorious roué named Androlio. Here the
serious plot joins the comic underplot which is already in progress.
Androlio has been hoping to seduce Amiana, daughter of a nobleman Basilonte, but her goal is marriage, and thus she refuses to
consent to anything less. While waiting for her to weaken, he

[19] Harbage, p. 214.

wastes no time in urging his cronies to accede to a mutual sharing of all sexual conquests. In the expectation that Orco will concur, he lets him go alone to serenade a mysterious advocate's daughter. Little does he know that the anonymous lady is Amiana, who, fearing detection of her amour at home, begs Orco to take her to Androlio's home. When Orco summons Androlio to his house to fetch her, he leaves Claramante alone, who gladly flees, fearing her "protector's" importunate demands. Amiana also disappears. While the two libertines accuse each other of deliberate deception, Orgemon is hastening away with Claramante. Their escape is never made. Androlio, disguised in a vizard, overtakes them, binds Orgemon to a tree, and rides off with Claramante. While he puts her into the dubious care of the lusty old Marilla, Dorando rescues Orgemon, and the two men vow to aid each other in love, little realizing that they both love the same woman. For two more acts these events continue to increase an audience's puzzlement. There are more disguises, duels, revelations, and recognitions until the play's joyous conclusion when Amiana and Androlio are matched, and Orgemon, who learns he is the brother of both Dorando and Amiana, successfully claims the hand of Claramante.

Harbage states that this play owes its ultimate source to the *Capa y Espada* drama of Spain, explaining that most of its plot materials can be found in Lope de Vega's *La Noche de San Juan*.[20] To be sure, it does belong to the comedy of intrigue genre, already mentioned earlier with regard to its Spanish extractions. Then, too, as Montague Summers has already noted,[21] it might well be in debt to Fletcher's *The Chances,* produced around 1620, and founded on a novel by Cervantes in his *Novelas Ejemplares.* In that play there is a Don John and a Don Frederick, who spend most of their time wenching. In character and interests, they are very similar to Androlio and Orco. They even suspect the other of intriguing with a female just as Orco and Androlio each believe the other is deceiving by keeping his amours confidential. Also there is a veiled lady, Constantia, who implores Don Frederick's

20 Page 215.
21 Montague Summers, "Introduction" to B. Van Thal's edition of Sir Samuel Tuke's *The Adventure of Five Hours*, p. xvii.

aid when she is planning an elopement with the Duke, and he assists her by taking her into his home for her protection. This is certainly reminiscent of the veiled Amiana, who, when wishing to be with Don Androlio, finds herself in Orco's home after having asked for his aid. Moreover, Constantia has a jealous brother Petruchio, just as Claramante is burdened with Leonte. Both brothers are overly eager to duel for their sister's honor, and in doing so they generally add to her distresses. In addition, the hapless Constantia is entrusted to the custody of Dame Gillian, an old woman who is always being teased by the impudent youth, upon whom she eventually seeks revenge. Similar in *The Distresses* is the episode wherein Androlio puts Claramante under the close charge of Marilla, an old woman whom he enjoys taunting. Knowing Davenant's affection for Fletcher's comedy, it is not likely that he was influenced by *The Chances* when he wrote *The Distresses*. Even the brevity of the title may not be coincidental.

The battle of the sexes as represented in the intrigue comedy provides a hearty serving of comic irony. The idea of two young ladies fleeing from their own homes to that of their lovers in search of protection fills the reader with amused anticipation for the brutal awakening such naiveté will receive. It is more surprising still that Orgemon should entrust his own beloved to the custody of his friend Androlio, whom he should surely recognize as a debauchée with no fixed principles regarding the pursuit of women. In addition, irony is most pronounced when two brothers, unaware of their kinship, promise to aid each other in securing the woman whom they do not realize is in reality the same woman. Yet for all this dramatic irony that titillates the curiosity, there is no ironic touch quite so comical as the intentional irony at the beginning of Act Five when Androlio, an avowed sinner of the deepest dye, though cheerfully immoral, complains of the wicked world in which he is forced to exist. But then, there is nothing comic in this play that is so successful as Davenant's creation of this witty, sarcastic town-gallant.

The dashing libertines of Restoration drama appeared in English drama long before the Restoration, having come into existence upon the stage because of their counterparts that infested London society. But they were seldom if ever portrayed dramatically as an ideal of masculine life. Nor is Androlio in *The Distresses* pictured as an example to be followed. Yet in considering his wit and repartee, often brilliant, and the delightful impertinence with which he plans a seduction, one would not hesitate to affirm that Davenant did find him a most agreeable type. Perhaps Androlio is much like Fletcher's Mirabell in *The Wild Goose Chase,* preferring to be a roué than a married man, but certainly he is well on his way to resembling the dubiously cynical Mirabell in Congreve's master comedy. Like Congreve's hero, he is so frankly licentious that we gladly wish him well in his impudent designs. Amiana does not interest him as a bride, but she would interest him in bed, and he is honest enough to tell her so. Nor is he too scrupulous to ask his comrades to share their mistresses in common. He can even in jest, somewhat tastelessly, offer his own sister though she be but three years old, whom one "may'st catch . . . with a cherry" (IV, 296). And yet for all his machinations, he is not really dangerous. The disguised Claramante does not interest him so much that news of another girl does not divert him. He enjoys all forms of exciting adventure, and the most exciting the moment offers is what he follows, whether it be a new female or the pursuit of runaway lovers. He himself explains his chief interest when referring to why he made a raid in the woods as a masked figure:

> 'Twas a kind of wicked wantonness,
> A pretty sort of doing mischief a
> Fine new way; th' old way of sinning is tedious. (IV, 327)

Thus he is not so interested in sinning as in having others realize that he is doing so with art. No wonder he reminds one of a Wildean character when he spouts such a choice epigram as "Patience is one of the seven deadly virtues" (IV, 335). Nor is this his only brilliant statement. Occasionally he is crude in his remarks, but more often, when an effective sparring partner is available, he delights in a verbal duel. His skill warrants this passion, as evinced in the wit combat he enjoys with Amiana and Orco:

Orco: Don Androlio! So early up! Studying,
I hope, to put your money out
To charitable uses.

Andr: 'Faith that will hardly be,
Till your diseases, Orco, drive you to
An hospital. I would thou hadst as many
As might destroy an over-grown city,
The Turk's grand army, or a wind-bound fleet;
You thrive like other traitors in this age,
And signify your greatness, by ent'ring everywhere
Without the mean civility of knocking.

Orco: I bring my powerful charter in my hand;
Abhor me! if thy mistress be not grown
A desperate wit. And, since the last
Digestion of her grief, she feels it prettily.

Andr: She'll fool me prettily, indeed, if this
Old toy of matrimony hold. Are you grown a wit, Amiana?

Amia: I shall be thought so, sir,
When I have reach'd capacity enough
To make you virtuous.

Andr: Nay, Y'are a wit! I find it by the great variety
Of posies, which you sent this morn for wedding rings.

Amia: As subtle and as wise a spirit as
You are, those silly charms are likely to
Prove strong enough to keep you long and fast
I'th' circle of mine arms, when once the priest
Shall conjure you.

Orco: Those vows, Androlio, which we make
At midnight, should,
In my opinion, not prove good i' th' common law,
Wer't not for that wanton worm – thy conscience –
Which still lies wriggling up and down thy breast,
Thou might'st be well excused, consid'ring too
The easiness and rawness of thy youth. (IV, 346-347)

It is this conversation that continues into a brief bargaining scene
that is in tone and substance very much in the Restoration manner:

Andr: E'en as she please. For my part, sir, I will
Deal plainly with her like an honest man;
Which is, to tell her, being married, I
Shall prove a very rogue.

Orco: I think thou wilt,
Unless her better grace preserve thee.

Andr: I shall often put you, Amiana, to
      Your morning's draught of tears; and to
      Your meal of sighs, on fasting nights, which will,
      I guess, be every night, according to
      My usual strict severity of life.
Amia: I will take order then, that you shall sigh for company.
Orco: Which, with a mutual groan or two, will make
      Rare music. When her treble's join'd unto
      Your bass, together with the cradle concordance
      Of three small organists; I mean, your children. (IV, 347-348)

Restoration wit meant raillery and repartee, often verging on the unmentionable, and this is the sort of wit which fits Androlio so securely. And like the wit of Etherege, it reveals a tendency to subdue human feelings in favor of an intellectual exercise, though, in close comparison to Etherege, it is still seen to exist on a stronger emotional level. Androlio's dialogue sparkles spontaneously, and in doing so, it betrays the basic warmth of character he prefers to hide.

The other elements of humor in the play are of a less sophisticated nature, adhering more to the coarse comedy that had been popular for generations. Such are the jokes made by musicians regarding a certain chambermaid and her freedom with a chamberpot (IV, 298). It is more protracted, however, in the short episodes concerning Marilla, an old woman to whom Androlio entrusts Claramante. When annoyed, Androlio chides her with the ungenerous accusation that when he was a mere child, "a foot high", she would have seduced him (IV, 335). Instead of noting the jest, the foolish old woman takes him seriously and attempts to persuade others that she had no "mind to his lordship in his cradle". Her pride being wounded, she has her revenge at the play's conclusion when she charges Androlio with rape:

Orco: Your rebel-man is here, Androlio!
      Brought by Officers, at this old gentlewoman's
      Complaint, for committing a rape.
Mari: Yes, truly, sir, down in the vault, towards
      The left corner by the garden stairs. I've cause
      To remember the place.
Andr: Ay, thou'lt ne'er forget a good turn.
Basi: How's that? a rape!

Mari: It had been so, forsooth, had I not yielded,
    As they say, to prevent harm.   (IV, 362)

As the dialogue reveals, Androlio accepts her indictment merrily, but then there is no reason for him to fret. The idea of an old frump desiring to involve herself in such a scandal is too delightfully incongruous to evoke anything but laughter. And doubtlessly the "commission of bedrid judges" will follow suit.

The "intrigue" of *The Distresses* is too involved for it to be a successful play. Inflated dialogue is another impediment. But for its kinship with the Restoration comedy of manners, it is of value. The insouciant spirit of light immorality that prevails occasionally whets the appetite for the comedies to come. Chiefly, however, it is the character of Androlio, one of Davenant's best comic creations, that satisfies. When he is present, all dullness disappears. Little more could a Restoration roué desire.

THE FIRST DAY'S ENTERTAINMENT AT RUTLAND HOUSE

After a long hiatus caused by the many events of the Interregnum which prevented him from writing drama, in 1656 Davenant presented the first licit performance of a play. Named *The First Day's Entertainment at Rutland House* for the mansion in Aldersgate Street where it was produced, it was designated an "opera", the foreign word being used to replace the offensive-sounding "theatre" or "play".

Little need be said about its amateurish production other than that hired declaimers and singers, abetted by music and song, presented two extended dialogues. The first dealt with a discussion of the case for public entertainment. Diogenes, the cynic, advocated the views of a Roundhead, which were boldly opposed by Aristophanes. The second dialogue, which concerns us here, was presented by a Londoner and a Parisian, who declaimed concerning the preeminence of their respective cities. In doing so they voiced Davenant's impressions of the two capitals which he had had plenty of opportunity to acquire. Because he could be so delightfully objective in his appraisals, his conclusions are often startlingly true, even today, and richly comic.

The Parisian spoke first, and bitingly so, on such topics as London buildings, English methods of education, and football. Even smoking was of concern. It was little more than half a century since tobacco had been introduced to England, yet it evidently took a secure hold on the habits of London society.

... yet I will enter, and therein oblige you much, when you know my aversion to the odour of a certain weed that governs amongst your coarser asquaintance, as much as lavender amongst your coarser linen; to which, in my apprehension, your sea-coal smoke seems a very Portugal perfume. I should here hasten to a period, for fear of suffocation, if I thought you so ungracious as to use it in public assemblies; and yet I see it grow so much in fashion, that me-thinks your children begin to play with broken pipes instead of corals, to make way for their teeth. You will find my visit short, I cannot stay to eat with you, because your bread is too heavy, and you disdain the light sustenance of herbs. Your drink is too thick, and yet you are seldom over-curious in washing your glasses. (III, 217-218)

It is doubtful that anyone would share such comments today on Englishmen's smoking habits, but more than one modern traveller would become even more scornful in commenting on English food and drink.

Certainly the criticism of English methods of education has not altered to any appreciable extent:

Before I leave you in your houses – where your estates are managed by your servants, and your persons educated by your wives – I will take a short survey of your children; to whom you are so terrible, that you seem to make use of authority whilst they are young, as if you knew it would not continue till their manhood. You begin to them with such rough discipline, as if they were born mad, and you meant to fright them into their wits again before they had any to lose. When they encrease in years, you make them strangers; keeping them at such distance, out of jealousy they should presume to be your companions, that when they reach manhood they use you as if they were none of your acquaintance. But we submit to be familiar with ours, that we may beget their affection before 'tis too late to expect it. If you take pains to teach them anything, 'tis only what they should not learn, bashfulness; which you interpret to be their respect towards you, but it rather shews they are in trouble, and afraid of you; and not only of you, but of all that are elder than themselves; as if youth were a crime, or, as if you had a greater quarrel to nature than to the devil: you seem to teach them to be ashamed of their persons, even then when you are willing to excuse their faults. ... This education you give them at home; but though you have frequently the pride to disdain the behavior of other nations, yet you have sometimes the discretion to send your sons abroad to learn it. To Paris they come, the school of Europe, where is taught the approaches and demeanours towards power: where they may learn honour, which is the generous honesty, which is the civil boldness of Courts. But there they arrive, not to converse with us, but with themselves; to see the gates of the Court, not to enter and frequent it or to take a hasty survey of greatness as far as envy, but not to study it as far as imitation. At last return home, despising those necessary virtues which they took not pains to acquire; and are only ill altered in their dress and mind, by making that a deformity in seeming overcareful and forced, which we make graceful in being negligent and easy. (III, 219-220)

Nevertheless, it is the Londoner who wins the debate. Armed with a more vicious wit, he levels his blows less thumpingly, though more incisively. Anyone who has had the occasion to take lodgings in a tenement or under a garret roof among "the poor people of Paris" will not deny the following assertion:

I will now visit your houses; which I confess transcendent as towers compar'd to the stature of those in our city; but as they are as high rooft as our belfries, so have they in them more than a noise of our bells; lodging distressed families in a room; and where there is no plenty, there is quietness. This chorus of clamour from several apartments will be sooner acknowledged when you consider that your nation affects no such brevity of speech as was practis'd by the Spartans, nor that majestical silence which is us'd by the Turks. But I accuse you of that of which you may take occasion to boast; because the stuffing of rooms with whole families denotes a populous city (III, 224-225)

Even the glories of the famed French cuisine are portrayed as something less than admirable:

Noise in your habitations of sleep is not so improper as your dead silence in the very regions of noise, your kitchens; where your cooks, though by education choleric and loud, are ever in profound contemplation, that is, they are considering how to reform the mistakes of nature in the original compositions of flesh and fish; she having not known, it seems, the sufficient mystery of hautgouts; and the production of their deep studies are sometimes so full of delicious fancy, and witty seasoning, that at your feasts when I uncover a dish, I think I feed on a very epigram. Who can comprehend the diversity of your pottages, carbonades, grillades, ragouts, haches, saupiquets, demi-bisques, bisques, capilotades, and entre-mets? But above all, I admire at the vast generation of your embroiderers of meat, your larders; their larding being likewise diversified from bacon of Mayence to porpoise of St. Malo; which, though it may be some cause of obliging and calling in the Jews, yet your perpetual persecution of that poor fish will so drive away the species from your coasts, as you will never be able to foretell a storm.   (III, 225-226)

Still the keenest stroke is the anecdote which reminds one of our own "After you my dear Alphonse" jibe, which refers to the senseless niceties of mythical French gallantry:

If I could reach your hand, I would endeavour to kiss it; for I should account myself worse bred than in a forest, if I had not learned a little from the abundant civility of Paris, where I have heard of two aged crocheteurs, heavy loaden with billets, who were so equally concerned in the punctilios of salutation, and of giving the way, that with the length of ceremony, "Monsieur c'est a vous, monsieur vous vous moques de vostre serviteur," they both sunk under their burdens, and so died, dividing the eternal honour of gentry education. (III, 228)

With this crushing compliment, the reader completes a type of debate that was never to end. We enjoy it as much today as Pepys did then.[22] In 1674 James Howard, in a play *The English Monsieur*, pictured an English character called Frenchlove who complained incessantly of English food, English respect of parents, and English beauties. With differing dramatic twists, playwrights were to continue exploiting French-English grievances, generally on a comic plane. In this "opera" Davenant was introducing to a London society, freshly familiar with French life, a subject of amusement that Restoration audiences would continue to find diverting.

A chronological reassessment of the dramas discussed in this chapter reveals that Davenant, although seldom secure in mixing comedy

----

[22]   Pepys' entry for February 7, 1664.

with tragedy, did have a talent for the task. After some initial fumbling, wherein he displayed more courage than taste, he managed in *Love and Honour* to achieve a comprehensive single-ness of impression that would do credit to the best playwrights of his age. Such success, however, he was not to maintain. Davenant cared more for his audience's approval than he did for history's estimation. And because his audience's theatrical tastes suffered from an excess of private interests, he necessarily sacrificed his own abilities. Ironically, such sacrifices rarely reaped the acclaim he desired. He was usually falling between two stools, either mixing the genres well and boring his audience, or entertaining his audience and violating the rules for esthetic dramatic development. Dramatically, Davenant well illustrates the adage that a man cannot serve two masters.

V

COMEDY IN DAVENANT'S TRANSLATIONS
AND ADAPTATIONS

When Davenant assumed the managership of the Duke's Play-house in the summer of 1660, it was to be expected that his previous care for his audience's whims would be intensified. Considering the competition of the only other monopoly company, the King's Company, which initially presented more brilliant actors,[1] Davenant had to avail himself of the soundest methods that would attract a favorable following to his theatre. The most important of these was to obtain proprietary rights for as many of the established native English plays as possible. Once this was done, he decided to alter them to suit his patrons, sensibly realizing that what suited a member of Elizabeth's court would scarcely please the more polished, and less serious, courtiers who sought the smiles of Charles II. Shakespeare's plays were not so sacrosanct in the seventeenth century as they are today, and so Davenant, with a keen eye on his box office receipts, would not have the slightest qualm in doctoring a *Macbeth* or *Measure for Measure* in order to heal his own financial wounds. In addition there were foreign plays to be translated, particularly since many in his audience had developed an affection for the French theatre during those long years of forced exile in Paris. One French playwright who particularly pleased was Molière, one whom Davenant was to import,

---

[1] Leslie Hotson, *The Commonwealth and Restoration Stage* (Cambridge, Mass., 1928), p. 242. Professor Hotson devotes two chapters to a detailed discussion of the success and merits of these two companies. Thorough research on this subject is to be found also in Eleanore Boswell, *The Restoration Court Stage 1660-1702* (Cambridge, Mass., 1932).

thereby initiating an influence that was to have an increasing emphasis in the decades to come.[2]

THE PLAYHOUSE TO BE LET

The French playwright's *Sganarelle, ou le Cocu Imaginaire* (1660),[3] a lively farce on a cuckold theme, became the subject of Act Two in his composite piece *The Playhouse to be Let,* otherwise studied in Chapter Three of this book. Although the Maidment and Logan edition of Davenant's works says that all the dramatic pieces of this work, with the exception of the first act, were written in the time of Oliver Cromwell,[4] it is unlikely that this Molière playlet was translated at a time before it appeared in France. May 28th is the date of its first Paris production,[5] and on May 29th Charles II celebrated his thirtieth birthday by making his triumphal return to London.[6] In any case it did not appear on the English stage until the summer of 1663.

The French play deliberately contrives a plot so that jealousy, presented as being entirely unwarranted, will appear an inherently ridiculous emotion. Four main people are involved: Sganarelle, the imaginary cuckold; his wife; Célie, the daughter of one Gorgibus; and her suitor Lélie. Célie, unhappy because her irate father wishes to marry her to an uglier and wealthier man than Lélie, to whom she was originally promised, faints while gazing at a picture of her lover. At this moment the luckless Sganarelle spots her distress and rushes forth to help. As he places his hand on the young lady's breast to test her breathing, his suspicious wife, seeing him, thinks the worst. Later Sganarelle comes upon his wife gazing at Lélie's picture, which has been left behind on the ground, and he

---

[2]   See John Wilcox, *The Relation of Molière to Restoration Comedy* (New York, 1938).

[3]   The edition of Molière used for this study was *Œuvres de Molière*, ed. Eugene Despois (Paris, 1875), II.

[4]   Davenant, IV, 3.

[5]   Molière, II, 137.

[6]   Nethercot, *Sir William D'Avenant, Poet Laureate and Playwright-Manager* (Chicago, 1938), p. 343.

hastily interprets it as signifying his sprouting horns. Following a noisy altercation, Sganarelle is left alone with the picture in his hand; at this moment Lélie returns from his extended voyage at sea. Having heard that his fiancée has been betrothed to a mean-featured man during his absence, he immediately assumes that Sganarelle is the one. Despondent, he receives the solicitations of the Wife, a kindness that does not arouse sympathy from her choleric husband. To complicate the mistaken impressions, Célie learns, through Sganarelle's statements, that her lover is involved elsewhere, and thus in tears she submits to her father's will. In time we learn that Célie, because of her betrothed's surprise marriage to another, is to be released from her father's promise, but not before Sganarelle, clothed in armor, foolishly attempts to defend his honor. At the conclusion the simple moral that one is not to believe all that one sees is eagerly affirmed by everyone involved, and the amusing complications end in a merry song and dance.

The most salient change made in Davenant's translation of the original Molière is the use of a quasi-French dialect. The opening lines read thus:

Célie: Ah tinke not myn art vill consant to dat.
Gorg: Doe you grom-bell littel impertinant?
    Vat, vould your young fantasque braine govarne mi
    Raison paternell? Vich sold give de law
    De fader or de chile? You sold be glad
    Of such a husband. You will say you be ignorant
    Of his humeur, bute you know he is rish,
    He has terty tousant duckat, and derefore
    Is honest gentill man.
Célie: Helas! my arte! (IV, 33-34)

Throughout the rest of the play this scarcely authentic dialect is maintained. Upon occasion the listener is surprised to hear inflections that are more characteristic of Italian speech patterns than of the French. In answering the angry wife, Célie says, "speaka boldly", and a few speeches later the servant has the line, "Make response in order and leta me speak' '(IV, 45). One may even detect a somewhat Swedish lilt to occasional phrasing, particularly

as it appears on the printed page in such an utterance as Sganarelle's, "Begarr! dis be true as de sun shina / Dat I may be marry'd
to myn vife" (IV, 46). Davenant certainly had no compunctions
about accuracy in suggesting a foreign French accent. His goal
was to amuse. Some twenty-five years earlier, in depicting Bumble,
the Dutch sea captain in *News from Plymouth*, he realized the
benefit of exaggerating the characteristics and national idiosyncrasies of foreigners. Now, with an audience that had spent many
years in France, most of whom would have had mixed feelings
about their hosts, he could again capitalize on this theatrical device. And doubtlessly the atrocious accent spoken in this play was
quite hilarious.

Davenant also felt it necessary to accelerate the plot development in order to compress the play into dimensions suitable to one
act. He did this both by shortening speeches and excising entire
scenes. Yet, whenever he economized, Davenant always saved the
sense of a speech. In Molière, when Gorgibus is instructing his
daughter as to why she must marry the suitor he has selected, he
speaks at length:

> Lui fût-elle engagée encore davantage,
> Un autre est survenu dont le bien l'en dégage.
> Lélie est fort bien fait; mais apprends qu'il n'est rien
> Qui ne doive céder au soin d'avoir du bien;
> Que l'or donne aux plus laids certain charme pour plaire,
> Et que sans lui le reste est une triste affaire.
> Valère, je crois bien, n'est pas de toi chéri;
> Mais, s'il ne l'est amant, il le sera mari.
> Plus que l'on ne le croit ce nom d'époux engage,
> Et l'amour est souvent un fruit du mariage.
> Mais suis-je pas bien fat de vouloir raisonner
> Où de droit absolu j'ai pouvoir d'ordonner?
> Trêve donc, je vous prie, à vos impertinences;
> Que je n'entende plus vois sottes doléances.
> Ce gendre doit venir vous visiter ce soir:
> Manquez un peu, manquez à le bien recevoir!
> Si je ne vous lui vois faire fort bon visage,
> Je vous ... Je ne veux pas en dire davantage.   (Scene I) [7]

[7]   Footnoting for the Molière play will include only the scene number.

As handled by Davenant, only five lines of dialogue are necessary:

> Lélie is vell accomplis, bute all ting
> Must submit to de good occasion of
> Riches; de rishe person vill come dis nite,
> If I see you regard him vit de helas
> I sall – vell, I say no more.   (IV, 34)

By omitting the ethical platitudes and accompanying garrulities of expression, Davenant somewhat alters and weakens his characterization of the father; nevertheless, he is uninterested in a developed character. It is farcical incident that is of importance, and thus only the essential substance of an address is necessary.

Sometimes excessive cutting lessens the comedy. When Sganarelle sees his wife gazing at the picture of Lélie, he tears it from her with a brief admission of his offended ego:

> Is not myn morsell sufficiant to
> Stay your stomach, but must you taste de
> Haut gout of a gallant.   (IV,36)

In Molière, on the other hand, the buffoon's outraged vanity is increased, with an added effect of comic purpose:

> Et, de par Belzébut, qui vous puisse emporter,
> Quel plus rare parti pourriez-vous souhaiter?
> Peut-on trouver en moi quelque chose à redire?
> Cette taille, ce port que tout le monde admire,
> Ce visage si propre à donner de l'amour,
> Pour qui mille beautés soupirent nuit et jour;
> Bref, en tout et partout, ma personne charmante
> N'est donc pas un morceau dont vous soyez contente?
> Et pour rassasier votre appétit gourmand,
> Il faut à son mari le ragoût d'un galand?   (Scene VI)

Of greater loss is the comic irony which is occasionally diminished by such foreshortening. An instance of this is when Sganarelle, not without fears for his own safety, decides that he must exact revenge. The English dramatist has him say:

> De cuckol-maker may be muche valiant,
> And lay de baston on de back as he doe lay de
> Horn on mi head. He may kill me;
> 'Tis better to ave de horn den no life.

> If my vife has done injure, let her grieve:
> Vy soud I cry dat doe no rong? But agen
> I begin to be sensible and vill ave de vengeance,
> And soundely, vor I vill virst tell de vorlt
> Dat he ly vit myn vife.   (IV, 42)

Molière devotes fifty-eight lines to the same account, the extra verbiage greatly extending the ironic possibilities of Sganarelle's timid bravado. No more than the beginning of his speech is necessary to express the difference:

> Doucement, s'il vous plaît! Cet homme a bien la mine
> D'avoir le sang bouillant et l'âme un peu mutine;
> Il pourroit bien, mettant affront dessus affront,
> Charger de bois mon dos comme il a fait mon front.
> Je hais de tout mon cœur les esprit colériques,
> Et porte grand amour aux hommes pacifiques;
> Je ne suis point battant, de peur d'être battu,
> Et l'humeur débonnaire est ma grande vertu.
> .... (Scene XXVII)

Although one finds it difficult to forgive the aesthetic loss to the play of such excisions, one should understand the necessities of them. Exigencies of time compression demanded that anything extraneous to the development of the plot must go. Considering this need, one willingly admits the competence of Davenant's pruning, for the speed of incident intrigue is skillfully met to yield the maximum of comic gusto.

The same requirement causes the excision of whole scenes. The first of these is the seventh scene in the Molière comedy. In it one Gros-René implores Lélie to satisfy his natural need for food and drink before undertaking an affair of the heart. To all such entreaties the eager lover turns a deaf ear. The scene is amusing, and it does serve to tease the spectator's curiosity regarding the plot development. But it is not directly of value to the central conflict; therefore it too disappears. A like fate befalls Molière's thirteenth and fourteenth scenes which are devoted to the Wife's relative's urging of Sganarelle to display less haste and more caution in his thirst for revenge. Its sole value is to impress further upon the spectator the absurdity of Sganarelle's rashness. Still it does have the accompanying weakness of hampering the English playwright's purpose of maintaining a rapidly-paced central action. Likewise, Scene Fifteen, containing the brief comic irony of Lélie's envy of Sganarelle, is deleted.

This same comic irony, so vital to Molière's work, is seriously devitalized in Davenant's only attempt to recast a scene. In Molière, Sganarelle is studying the portrait of Lélie when the latter enters. As the supposed cuckold vents his wrath, simultaneously ignoring what he considers the inquisitiveness of a stranger, the crestfallen Lélie, in spoken asides, voices his despondency. Here Molière toys with the spectator's eager anticipation of what will occur when Sganarelle recognizes the stranger as being the subject of the hated portrait. Davenant, unfortunately, precludes such suspense. In his version Sganarelle recognizes Lélie immediately, and they both continue at some length to speak in asides. Such an alteration, eschewing the suspense element, seriously impairs the comic vitality of the scene. Although it is simple to find substantial reasons why the English playwright was forced to reject comic irony elsewhere, there is no justification here at all. The scene is not appreciably shorter in the new version, nor does it cohere more closely to plot action. It is Davenant's only unforgivable error in this adaptation.

When, however, Davenant adds a line or two, not to be found in the original, it always succeeds in provoking a laugh. The first example of this is noticed when Sganarelle is summoned to assist Célie after she swoons in grief while gazing at Lélie's picture. In the French version he enquires thus:

> Madame, êtes-vous morte?
> Hays! elle ne dit mot.   (Scene III)

In the English translation it reads:

> Madame, tell me
> If you be dead. Hey! see say noting
> Can I believe her vit out her vorde?   (IV, 35)

The last line, akin to the inane comments of stage comedians today, makes Sganarelle appear even more stupid than he was formerly, not necessarily a characterization improvement, but it would certainly evoke a boisterous guffaw. Quickly succeeding this hilarious remark is the added statement, "Leta me feel a littel", which accompanies Sganarelle's laying of a hand on Célie's breast in order to determine her state of swoon. Such a remark, obviously designed to evoke a wicked smirk, speaks for the less subtle tastes of Davenant's audience. And on the next page of dialogue, when the outraged husband finds his wife with Lélie's picture, Davenant substitutes for "D'un fort vilain soupçon je me sens l'âme émue" (Scene VI) the expression, "I feel de littel horne on mi bro" (IV, 36). Thus he alludes more forcefully to the standard cuckold joke, long successful in pleasing an English audience, whether sophisticated or not.

A gift for using the topical and the colloquial, characteristic of Davenant's earlier comedies, is employed to increase one's humorous enjoyment. Such is to be seen in the likening of Célie with "live again / As de harang in de sea" (IV, 36), or in the bold though harmless curse of Sganarelle, "Figa for honour, I be rob of myn reputation / Vit de nabeurs" (IV, 41). The comic effect of such familiar expressions is to be found again in the topical allusion to a Roman Catholic custom, referred to in the Wife's vicious retort to Célie:

> You ave as mush conscience as de devil,
> Ven he be seeke vith eating on Fryday. (IV, 45)

Though only a part of Davenant's audience would be Roman Catholic, and some of them surreptitiously so, all would be familiar with its demands as a result of their exile in France, and therefore this kind of remark, tossed off in anger, would communicate directly to their thirst for titillation.

Occasionally in his translations and adaptations Davenant can be accused of adding a little smut in order to pander to the debauched tastes of his day. But only one instance of such a compromise appears in this play. In the French version, when Célie and Sganarelle are sympathizing mutually, the dialogue reads:

Célie: . . . .
> Dois-tu ne te pas croire indigne de la vie,
> Après t'être souillé de cette perfidie?
> O Ciel! est-il possible?

Sgana: Il est trop vrai pour moi.
Célie: Ah! traître! scélérat! âme double et sans foi!!
Sgana: La bonne âme!
Célie: Non, non, l'enfer n'a point de gêne
       Qui ne soit pour ton crime une trop douce peine.
Sgana: Que voilà bien parler!
Célie: Avoir ainsi traité
       Et la même innocence et la même bonté!
Sgana: (Il soupire haut) Hay!
Célie: Un cœur qui jamais n'a fait la moindre chose
       A mérité l'affront où ton mépris l'expose! (Scene XVI)

In the English adaptation this same passage contains some bold insertions:

Célie: O, Even! Is it possibel dat he tink
       To live after dis perfidie?
Sgana: Madam, he is not dying: he is steal vay
       To eat de good pottage to make him abel
       To make me more cuckol.
Célie: At traitre! vicked man vit dobill art
       End vit no soul.
Sgana: Mi not know if he have soul, bute mi
       Vife be acquainted vit his body.
Célie: No torture is sufficient vor his grand crime!
       He deserve to ly on de rack.
Sgana: He do ly already at rack an manger.
       But dat doe him good and me hurt.
Célie: Helas! de inconstancy!
Sgana: Hey! But de sign vit out revange be
       To no more propose den de bray of de ass.
Célie: Ah, injure de art dat never vas infidel. (IV, 41)

The coarsely comic note here, entirely absent in the original, is surely good for a hearty reaction from an audience wanting levity of speech, and yet it is by no means offensive. When compared to the products of Davenant's contemporaries, this addition is mild indeed.

Notwithstanding the Elizabethan-like song and dance that is added to end his version, Davenant, in his adaptation, does not equal the French master of comedy. The mock-French dialect is little compensation for the satire that Molière emphasized. Surely even the farcical touches possess a more artistic aspect in the original. Davenant's Sganarelle is too gross in his absurdity, more akin to the foolish rustics presented years earlier in the subplot of his own tragedy *The Cruel Brother*. When one considers, however, the necessity of time element and the Restoration audience, one would certainly admit that for a practical-minded producer this adaptation is the more resourceful.

THE LAW AGAINST LOVERS

Over a year was to pass before Samuel Pepys would enter in his diary for February 18, 1662, the following:

> ... I went to the opera, and saw the "Law against Lovers", a good play, and well performed, especially the little girl's (whom I never saw act before) dancing and singing; and were it not for her, the losse of Roxalana would spoil the house.

One is tempted to believe that Pepys' predilection for dancing girls betrayed him into believing that Davenant's first adaptation of a Shakespeare play was a good one. There are some fairly skillful features about it, particularly the interweaving of the Benedick and Beatrice subplot from *Much Ado About Nothing* with the main plot of *Measure for Measure,* but on the whole any serious comparison with the originals illustrates beyond doubt that one may tamper with Shakespeare, but one cannot better him.

To ally the two plots Benedick becomes the younger brother of Angelo, and Beatrice is the latter's ward. The problem of Claudio remains the same, soon enlisting in this version the sympathetic services of both Benedick and Isabella. The latter appeals to Angelo and receives in return the same offer that Shakespeare designed for this cold deputy. Unlike his predecessor, however, Davenant does not have Claudio beg Isabella to save him; rather the young lover, in requesting his sister to care for the hapless Julietta, resigns himself to his punishment. Nevertheless, the pregnant girl will not submit so readily. She suggests that Isabella comply with Angelo's request, to which she receives the harsh retort that if Claudio's life matters so much then she, Julietta, under disguise, will keep the assignation. This is the only reference to Shakespeare's Mariana story, which is otherwise, and not regretfully, deleted. After further complications in which Beatrice keeps urging Benedick to force Claudio's release, the playgoer is appalled to learn that Angelo's corrupt proposition to Isabella was merely motivated by a wish to test her virtue. Following this unconvincing surprise comes the complex results of Benedick's armed revolt against his older brother and the supposed execution of Claudio, both being almost entirely Davenant's own work. At the conclusion the Duke appears to bestow a general amnesty, pairing off the lovers so evenly that the chaste Isabella is matched with a completely incredible Angelo.

As mentioned earlier, the Mariana episode is absent, the most obvious omission. Since Davenant's interest in comedy is our only concern here, however, what appears to be a more serious omission is the mirthful behavior of the scurrilous Pompey, Froth, and Elbow. Nor does Mistress Overdone appear, and her presence is lamented for two desirable reasons. She provides motivation for Angelo's revival of a forgotten law. And there is some rich comic irony in this bawdy crone's selfish concern for her own welfare while being immersed in a profession where she obviously has no concern for the welfare of more helpless beings. As with many of Shakespeare's minor characters, the laughter evoked by her behavior proves indirectly moral. Mistress Overdone's loss is not a small one.

When Davenant does appropriate comic scenes and characters from Shakespeare, they are altered. This is most evident in the depiction of two of Shakespeare's wittiest lovers, Benedick and Beatrice, wherein a great deal of their former wit has either been omitted or replaced. An excellent example of this concerns the tart-tongued lovers in Act One. Beatrice's first entrance is with Julietta and Balthazar, characters belonging to *Much Ado About Nothing*, and Viola, an addition of Davenant's own. Here Beatrice's enquiries regarding Benedick resemble those contained in Shakespeare's play. Yet, with the first line of her dialogue, we note a difference that is to become more marked as the play progresses. In Davenant the girl asks, "Does Signior Benedick return tonight"

(V, 119), whereas in Shakespeare the question reads, "I pray you, is Signior Mountanto returned from the wars, or no" (I, i). Signior Mountanto, derived from a fencing term, means "Signior Thruster", a clever quip that may be deliberately ambiguous. In any case it can be so interpreted and still be in keeping with Beatrice's personality. But such a remark does veer towards the obscure, an obscurity that is perhaps more noticeable in Beatrice's next elaborate jest about challenging Cupid, also deleted here; for a playwright who strove to achieve clarity of meaning, this obscurity was not welcome. Only that dialogue could be saved which was directly pertinent to the hybrid plot devised.

Then, too, some of the dialogue preserved is given to other characters, such as Beatrice's sharp retort to the observation, "I see, lady, the gentleman is not in your books" (I, i). Whereas Beatrice originally answered, "No, an he were, I would burn my study", this reply is given to Viola and becomes, "If he were, I have heard my sister say / She would burn her Study" (V, 120). Obviously, by transferring the line, so that it involves two persons, rather than being focused on one as in the original, it loses its brightness of repartee. Undoubtedly, Davenant had an actress who could sing and dance, and he wanted both in this production. If he was to give her dialogue as well, then Beatrice must share her own role. No other reason can justify this transference of dialogue, for in doing so Beatrice's vigor as an independent woman is severely diminished.

Another revision is to have Beatrice hide behind a curtain immediately before Benedick's first appearance. Usually when an actor deliberately eavesdrops on another in a comedy, the spectator, in knowing that the actor speaking is ignorant of being overheard, expects a certain comic irony. This irony can be most amusing. But such is not the purpose here. For no evident reason the playwright wants the ladies absent when more exposition regarding Angelo's new decree is to be given. Then, when Beatrice does return, because she cannot adequately hear the conversation on stage, no further mention is made of her hiding. Thus the spectator's anticipation of comedy comes to nothing, and he feels cheated.

When this heroine returns the two lovers immediately launch into the "Lady Disdain" verbal battle that is so delightfully arch in Shakespeare's version. In Davenant the substance is the same, but by pruning the wit, he loses its former lustre. For example, in Shakespeare the dialogue begins as follows:

Bene: What, my dear Lady Disdain! Are you yet living?
Beat: Is it possible Disdain should die while she hath
such meet food to feed it as Signior Benedick?
Courtesy itself must convert to disdain if you
come in her presence.
Bene: Then is courtesy a turncoat. But it is certain
I am loved of all ladies, only you execpted. And
I would I could find in my heart that I had not a
hard heart, for truly I love none.   (I, i)

When truncated it means the same perhaps, but the pleasure provided by verbal dexterity is absent:

Bene: My dear Lady disdain! are you yet living?
Beat: Can disdain die when she has so fit food
To feed it as Benedick?
Bene: I am belov'd of all ladies, only
You excepted; and I am sorry they must lose
Their sighs; for I have a hard heart,
And can love none.   (V, 123)

This debilitation of the Comic Spirit is furthered by Davenant's own addition to this scene just prior to the play's conclusion:

Viol: Y'are welcome home, my lord. Have you brought
Any pendants and fine fans from the wars?
Bene: What, my sweet bud, you are grown to a blossom!
Viol: My sister has promis'd me that I shall be
A woman, and that you shall make love to me,
When you are old enough to have a wife.
Bene: This is not a chip of the old block, but will prove
A smart twig of the young branch.   (V, 124)

Not only is the humor of these botanical metaphors almost nil, but by having them addressed to Viola, attention toward Beatrice is diverted. Considering the puerility of such lines, perhaps for Beatrice's sake it is just as well.

Throughout the rest of the scenes concerning Benedick and Beatrice, similar misfortunes occur, Some of Benedick's best lines, like Beatrice's, are transferred, this time to Lucio and Balthazar. Worse still is the loss of the wonderfully comic irony when Benedick, who has just boasted of his independence of love, swiftly succumbs to it while overhearing Leonato, Claudio, and Don Pedro speak of Beatrice's passion for him. Similarly, except for a speech or two, most of Beatrice's contemptuous remarks to Leonato on marriage, most ironically received by the spectator, are removed. In short, little comic irony remains in this new depiction of two of Shakespeare's most memorable comic characters. When they are together, they are more apt to be discussing plot details, such as the episode of the signet ring or the desire to free Claudio. Such bantering as does occur between them is too weak to evoke much audience response. Therefore they seldom seem to exist for the purpose of comic characterization alone; rather they exist to serve plot.

Comic irony does exist elsewhere in this play. In one instance it is Davenant's own invention, and it concerns Beatrice. In Act Three, after Lucio pleads the cause of Benedick, Beatrice, in a playful mood, teasingly suggests that her devotion is directed towards Lucio. Rapidly this fellow, considerably elevated following his journey from Shakespeare to Davenant, shifts his cause, expounding his intention in seaman's language that is reminiscent of discourse in *News from Plymouth*:

Lucio: Sits the wind on that side? I must hoist sail,
With top, and top gallant.   (V, 156)

Knowing how little sincerity is present in Beatrice's flirtation, we are amused to hear Lucio deny the existence of Benedick's affection, claiming that he has spoken only in order to have an opportunity to speak for himself. At this point Beatrice leaves stage for no well-motivated reason. One can merely assume that the playwright wished to have Lucio alone with Balthazar so that he could pursue his comic irony, and this he does by revealing how eagerly Lucio anticipates the dowry that Beatrice will bring with her in marriage. This addition of Davenant's does have its mirthful moments, yet one would hardly see it as a satisfactory substitute for the ironic scenes that have been excised.

The one ironic scene concerning Lucio in *Measure for Measure*, that is, his slandering of the Duke to the disguised Duke himself, is maintained, though severely trimmed in length. Only a couple of Lucio's assertions regarding the Duke's amorous proclivities survive. Other references to political and religious weaknesses are dropped. And in Davenant, the insults are softened by Lucio's explanation that the Duke "began to steer / The right course about forty; but good man, / He repented the lost time of his youth" (V, 172). Rehabilitating Lucio has surely not agreed with his previously comic aspects. In addition, the comic surprise of Lucio unwittingly unmasking the Duke, along with his accompanying embarrassment, is almost entirely lost; in this version the Duke simply tells a somewhat chagrined Lucio that he was the disguised friar to whom Lucio had boastfully spoken. Such irony as there is belongs rightly to Shakespeare. Unfortunately, too little of it remains.

Another comic incident from *Measure for Measure* that survives in mangled fashion is the Barnardine episode. For instance, Pompey is replaced by another bawd, this time anonymously designated as the Fool. With him the same problem occurs as in the corresponding Lucio story. What is comic belongs to Shakespeare, and yet much of the best comedy is omitted for reasons of irrelevance to plot and the harsh demands of playing time.

The most successful additions of Davenant consist of isolated lines that are, unfortunately, too infrequent, and most of them are familiar to anyone acquainted with his earlier dramas. A couple of these approach the coarse jest. When Viola enquires the reason for Julietta's punishment, the following is said:

Viola: Pray, sister, why is Juliet in prison?
Beat: Peace, Viola, you are too young to know.
Bene: She play'd with a bearded baby, mistress,
   Contrary to law.   (V, 136)

Again later, when Benedick reproves Lucio for wooing his Beatrice, Lucio denies it thus:

Lucio: I ever thought her a mermaid.
Bene: How so?
Lucio: From the breasts downwards she's as cold as a fish. (V, 166)

Neither remark is unduly obscene, no more than many appearing in his earlier plays, and yet for a playwright whose avowed intention was to purge the old plays of their scurrility, both remarks are too frank. Davenant was never to become consistent in his prudery. Too often, in his zeal, he censored coarsely accurate words, and then he would insert bawdy comments that had much less justification for their presence. Evidently he found it difficult to reconcile his duty to the injunction of the royal patent regarding levity of speech with his duty to his audience's thirst for the very same license.

His old vexation, the Platonic doctrine of love, is revived for satire in what belongs to Davenant's better contribution to the Benedick-Beatrice colloquy:

Bene: . . . .
. . . . But patience! and we shall
Have right when we are heard.
Beat: Heard? yes, may she,
Who henceforth listens to your sighing sex,
Have her ass-ears in public bor'd, as love's
Known slave, and wear for pendants, morrice-bells,
As his fantastic fool.
Bene: No whisp'ring the Platonic way?
Beat: Platonic way? my cousin has Plato'd it
Profoundly; has she not? i' th' name of mischief,
Make friendship with yourselves and not with us.
Let every Damon of you chuse his Pythias,
And tattle romantic philosophy
Together, like bearded gossips.
Bene: Though such conversation might breed peace in
A palace, yet 'twould make but a thin court. (V, 178)

Certainly the Platonic doctrine was not being observed at Charles II's court, but enough people would remember Henrietta Maria's foolish flirtation with it to make it worthy of resurrection.

This ability of Davenant's to provide welcome local color is again noticed in his jibe at the clergy:

Bene: You trip it too fast!
You need not be so swift to meet misfortune.
I had just now a letter from the Provost;
Who either suspects the truth of the pardon,

> Because I enjoin'd him to secrecy,
> Or else is led by a friar to some fresh design.
Beat: Are we circumvented by a friar?
> Rather than not vex that friar, I'll invent
> A new sect, and preach in a hat and feather.
Bene: 'Tis strange that men of their discretion
> Should come abroad in old fashion gowns,
> And drest with abominable negligence.
Beat: Bus'ness makes them great slovens, and they love
> To be busy.
Bene: And never observe
> The right seasons when they are necessary,
> For though we are content with their company
> When we are old and dying; yet methinks
> They should not trouble us with their good counsel
> When we are young, and in good health.   (V, 167)

Not only does this passage insult the clergy, surely no offence to a Restoration audience, but it does offer a welcome comment on the relaxed social attitude towards the church's function, most evident in the last speech of Benedick.

Curiously enough, the play ends with an example of grisly humor that is akin to the charnel-house jokes common to Vasco and Gridonell in Davenant's earlier plays:

Lucio: Fool, I've a mind to marry your grandmother.
Fool: She stays for you in the church, and will prove
> A sweet bed-fellow, for she has not been
> Buried above a month.   (V, 211)

Lying with a corpse is certainly an unattractive image with which to end this comedy, but it is characteristic of Davenant's inability to focus clearly on this play a single purpose. He wanted to ally two well-known Shakespeare plots, observing the classical unities, and elevating the moral tone. He wished also to entertain a highly homogeneous audience that did not care to be mentally taxed. Thus he proffered a complicated plot, several scenes of song and dance, and a few gobbets of such humor as he had supplied in earlier decades. Even without a comparison to Shakespeare, one is forced to admit that this play has only its "moments", and they are sparse indeed. It speaks well for Restoration audiences that

Downes was forced to relegate *The Law Against Lovers* to his list of minor and incidental plays.[8]

MACBETH

Before analyzing *The Rivals,* Davenant's next adaptation of a comedy, a few words might be said about his version of Shakespeare's tragedy *Macbeth*, which Pepys first saw and liked on November 5, 1664. For our purpose here it is solely of interest in that the justly famed scene of the porter and the knocking at the gate is omitted. All that remains is a servant's answer to Lennox' enquiry as to why he did not immediately reply to the knocking at the gate: "Labor by day causes rest by night" (V, 340). Although Davenant had valued the use of comic relief in earlier tragedies of his own, he evidently changed his opinion of its worth. Or perhaps he simply thought its presence rather incongruous in a tale that encompasses so much supernatural as well as natural horror. Obviously his audience did not object to its absence. The Davenant *Macbeth* immediately won a host of converts and was to continue its favored position on into the nineteenth century.[9]

THE RIVALS

Another adaptation that was to be heartily applauded was *The Rivals*, a somewhat skilled comedy that is generously based on Fletcher's tragedy *The Two Noble Kinsmen*.[10] Upon its first presentation in September, 1664, it ran for nine successive nights, and thereafter various revivals were offered.[11] Like *The Law Against Lovers*, it was to be patronized with pleasure by Samuel

---

8   Downes, *Roscius Anglicanus*, p. 26.

9   Nethercot, pp. 392-393.

10   A close comparison of the two plays is to be found in A. Krusenbaum, *Das Verhältnis von Davenants Drama The Rivals zu The Two Noble Kinsmen* (Halle, 1895). Also see A. C. Sprague, *Beaumont and Fletcher on the Restoration Stage* (Cambridge, Mass., 1926).

11   Nethercot, p. 389.

Pepys. Only on this occasion the noted diarist was to be more direct in his appreciation of the production's virtues. In his diary entry for September 10, 1664, Pepys gave his prime attention to one Gosnell, his own former housemaid and favorite, who "comes and sings and dances finely". For in this production, too, Davenant was to pander to more frivolous tastes by adding an abundance of songs, pageants, and dances, thus providing opportunities for actresses with musical talents.

Notwithstanding these appendages, Davenant's version appears to be more stageworthy than Fletcher's diffuse drama. In order to present it as a Resotration comedy, Davenant first adheres, though imperfectly to be sure, to the developing vogue for the classical unities. Most of the material in Fletcher's first act is omitted, such as the episode concerning three mourning queens, unsuited to comedy, and also the battle scene. Here, following the war, the drama begins, and it immediately concentrates on the extraordinary friendship of Philander and Theocles, formerly Palamon and Arcite. Throughout the remainder of the play, wherein the plot focuses on the two men's love for Heraclia, who corresponds to Fletcher's Emelia, there is little to divert the spectator's interest. The curious subplot of the Jaylor's daughter in Fletcher's drama becomes in this version more closely related to the main plot with the mad Daughter being replaced by Celania, a lady friend of Heraclia, and daughter to a Provost, thus making it possible for the happy hymeneals of both heroes at the conclusion. Nor does this famous tale of friendship sprawl any longer over the space of two kingdoms. It is now concentrated in the land of Arcadia, and it works itself out, as unity of time would desire, within a matter of a few days. Without doubt, this observance of the three unities does much to tighten the dramatic events and thereby channel an audience's interest more satisfactorily than would its predecessor.

An initial analysis of the play makes evident the playwright's debt to the love and honor motif which he has used in earlier dramatic efforts. The first departure from its predecessor in touching this motif comes at the conclusion of Act Two, immediately after Celania has freed Philander. Unlike the selfish Palamon, he is most concerned for the safety of Celania's father, fearing that his own freedom will mean the Provost's death. It is not until Celania assures him that the Prince of Arcadia will not forget her father's recent valor that he resolves to make sure his escape. Again, in Act Five, this same honor for another's welfare is displayed. Because Heraclia cannot decide which lover she prefers, the Prince of Arcadia has two strange men brought forth to denounce both Philander and Theocles. The injustice of this slander persuades both heroes to defend each other staunchly, and therefore the puzzled Heraclia is as baffled as ever as to which rival she shall choose. The dilemma of this love and honor theme is fortunately ended when Celania enters to claim her affection. Philander, having until this moment vowed his love for Heraclia, cavalierly transfers his ardor to the long suffering maiden who earlier effected his escape. In tragedy such a contrived conclusion would be unacceptable; in romantic comedy, it is entirely welcome.

In addition the comic mode of Spanish intrigue has left its mark on this alteration. Not quite two years before, London hailed Sir Samuel Tuke's *The Adventure of Five Hours* with its numerous adventures and complications, and the impact of its success was still an inspiration to eager producers. And in this mode Davenant had already practised his hand some twenty-five years earlier in his unsuccessful *The Distresses*. Combining his ability and theatrical acumen, he shrewdly doctored his alteration by adding to the already existing romantic difficulties the affair of Leucippe, Celania's maid, and Cunopes, the Provost's man, an affair which does not exist for itself alone, but is closely involved with the motivations of the central plot. As well, the stories of Heraclia and Celania are connected, unlike that of Emelia and the Jaylor's Daughter in *The Two Noble Kinsmen*, whose fates were entirely separated. When a subplot is separated from the main plot, as in Fletcher's tragedy, there is in moving from one story to the other a certain diffusion of the spectator's interest. In tragedy this can be most desirable in that it relaxes tension and provides relief from what might well be an intolerable emotional concentration. But in comedy a concentrated complexity of plot can often prove quite flattering to the spectator in demanding a sharp focusing of the mental faculties. And fans of Spanish intrigue enjoyed being so flattered. Thus, by enlarging the cast of characters and involving their respective destinies with that of the others, Davenant rigidly intensified his spectator's attention, providing the mental excitement his patrons enjoyed.

Earlier it was mentioned that the incident of the three mourning queens was erased because it violated unity of plot. Of greater importance is that it was alien to the Comic Spirit. For the latter reason Davenant excised or altered other aspects of Fletcher's tragedy. For example, the several scenes involving the two heroes, depicting the strife that has arisen between them, are not noticeably different from Davenant's source. And yet their bitterness seems less intense. By recasting their speeches in order to eliminate that which is unessential to meaning, by eschewing phrasing and words that appear too bold, he avoids the emotional mood generated in Fletcher's drama, and fortunately so. Emotion is always dangerous for comedy. Rather he maintains their strife on a level of artifice that speaks to our intellect only, supporting our satisfaction for the comic irony. Certainly this method is more in tune with the new conclusion. In Fletcher's version Arcite, victorious in his match with Palamon, falls from his horse and is wounded fatally. Before expiring he summons his former friend, gives him his bride, and then begs forgiveness. It is a romantic conclusion, obviously designed to evoke an emotional response. On the other hand, Davenant terminates his drama with everyone ending their problems happily, each benefiting from the blessings of the love and honor code. Nothing could be more artificial. Yet by expunging all suggestions of emotion, Davenant is able to present a plot that does not have a false ring. It never disturbs emotional truth, and it does serve that mental truth wherein all disbelief is suspended.

The other important concession to the Comic Spirit is Davenant's treatment of Celania. In Fletcher's drama the situation of the Jaylor's daughter is more pitiful. From the beginning Palamon, taking no notice of her at all, leaves her no hope. On the other hand, Celania at least has the satisfaction of knowing that Philander fears for the safety of her and her father. By elevating Celania socially, Davenant makes this possible. Then, too, when

Celania becomes distracted, hunger and fear aggravating her despair, her condition is not treated with the same sort of pathos as that which surrounds the Jaylor's daughter. From the time she first appears in the woods alone, the Daughter is given five scenes, at least three of them of considerable length. Swiftly her dementia develops, enlisting the anxious services of her father, a doctor, and of another wooer. With her final appearance on stage, although still not in complete control of her faculties, she is well enough to submit to the Wooer, on which occasion she requests plaintively that he be kind:

Daughter: But you shall not hurt me.
Wooer: I will not Sweet.
Daughter: If you do (Love) I'll cry. (V, ii)

The sad sentiment of these scenes remind one of those in which Ophelia is famed. However, in Davenant's treatment, one would never think of the unfortunate Ophelia. Not only is much less space given to Celania's scenes, but when she does appear, speaking lines that are similar in substance, though considerably shortened, the situation is such that her mental state never evokes our pity. The first scene in Act Four illustrates this difference. Formerly, in the Fletcher play, following a protracted serious discussion about her mental variance, the Daughter enters and converses with several characters who are anonymously designated as Brother, 1 Friend, and 2 Friend. These individuals are mere foils so that she may display the pathos of her situation. However, Davenant has his Celania deliver the same dialogue with Cunopes, a low comedy character he introduced earlier on several significant occasions. Because the audience has come to accept Cunopes as delightfully diverting, Celania's mental wanderings, when with him, never touch our hearts. In such a mood of merriment, the spectator does not accept her madness seriously and, therefore, when she returns quite sane at the play's conclusion, one is not surprised. Never once would the audience consider her dementia as anything more than temporary. To do otherwise would be to depart from the Comic Spirit.

Any scene in the original drama which could be suitably inserted in a comedy, Davenant retains, generally altering it to suit his purposes. For instance, the lighthearted episode wherein the two rivals temporarily forget their enmity in order to tease each other about past amours is present. In fact, it is expanded with a song by Theocles that suggestively winks at the too frequent result of lovers' careless dalliance. In addition, the country scenes are here, even though Gerrold, the schoolmaster, is absent. To these scenes has been added more pageantry, including a "Hunt in Musick" that begins the fourth act, in order to display the operatic trimmings that had become associated with Davenant's theatrical productions. One notes that to all of these country scenes Celania is connected. For this reason, as well as for shelving the colorfully Shakespearean schoolmaster, Davenant managed to keep his plot line less scattered than that of his source, without sacrificing seriously the rustic charm Fletcher had offered.

The most notable comic achievement of this play is Davenant's own, that of Cunopes and Leucippe, neither of whom was in the original. Cunopes, replacing the Gaol-keeper of Fletcher's drama, does serve the central plot. But, more important, he adds to the comic intrigue, while existing in his own right as a comical personality. He possesses a healthy objectivity that destroys our sympathies for excessive romanticism. When Philander despairs at some length following Theocles' amnesty, Cunopes has no respect for his wailings:

> You are tedious, sir!
> I would desire less of your tongue, good sir,
> And more of your ears, I have a charge to you. (V, 244)

This address replaces the corresponding one in Fletcher, which simply states, "My Lord for you / I have this charge too" (II, ii). A few lines later, when an angry Palamon says, "By this good light / Had I a sword I would kill thee", the Keeper retorts, "Why my Lord?" (II, ii). Cunopes, on the other hand, to the same threat haughtily proclaims, "I thank you!" (V, 244). Cunopes is a man to reckon with, for he has a remarkable independence of his own.

He is independent, in any case, until he falls in love. Then his state is described by Leucippe, the object of his wavering stability, in terms that remind one of the beguiled Malvolio:

> Yes, truly, he's grown the very farse!
> He lays aside his surly looks, and falls
> To fawning with a screw'd and mimic face,
> As if he had been tutor'd by an ape.
> He sings, and makes legs to the looking-glass;
> Is pleas'd with's face, because he smiles again. (V, 246)

In such a condition, he is fair game for Leucippe's design to covet the gaol keys, as her mistress Celania has requested so that she might free the prisoner, Philander. Later he is to regret his folly. Hidden from Leucippe's view, a situation always good for an audience's amusement, he overhears her uncomplimentary remark when she takes leave of her companion:

> Farewell! good Cunopes, if thou art hang'd
> Thou'lt meet this comfort at the fatal place,
> Hanging can never spoil so bad a face.
> Nurse Farewell.   (V, 254)

Nevertheless, his love is not to be daunted:

> Though she saw me not, she took her leave of me
> After the old phase; farewell, and be hang'd,
> Besides her commendations sent to my face.
> Those have good stomachs who can love the meat,
> Having been beaten with the spit. And yet
> I cannot hate her. There's some witch-craft in't! (V, 254)

This man has wit. And he is both more and less than a Malvolio. At times he is very much the low comedy character, close to a Jonsonian humor. At other times his incisive view of human dealings is about as sharp as that of a polished Restoration courtier. It is no wonder that in his succeeding scenes, wherein he is provided dialogue that Fletcher wrote for various subordinate figures, he often dominates the dialogue. As explained earlier, it is his vividness of color that prevents some of Celania's ravings from sinking into bathos. The most amusing figure in the play, he deserves to achieve his goal at the play's end.

Before leaving this play, one must note that in view of morals,

Davenant's version is purer than its predecessor. Except for the insertion of Theocles' song in his Act Three colloquy with Philander, and actually its bawdry is of the gentlest variety, much of Fletcher's crudity is censored. This is most evident in the transformation of the Daughter's plot. Undoubtedly one reason for this was Davenant's purported mission to purify the theatre. Nor could all of Fletcher's crudity mix comfortably with a comic tone. Nevertheless, Davenant does retain enough to keep his audience from being utterly starved for the commodity they expected. By emphasizing the lightly sophisticated and by unifying the plot, liberally embellishing it with music and dance, Davenant makes a happily stageworthy comedy out of Fletcher's unwieldy and uninteresting tragedy.

THE TEMPEST

Stageworthy is a term also to be applied to Davenant's adaptation, in collaboration with Dryden, of Shakespeare's *The Tempest*.[12] Abused as it has been, and sometimes justly, no one has ever attempted to argue that it is not theatrically effective. Following its successful presentation on November 17, 1667, it was within the next half year to receive at least five royal command performances.[13] It was to find great favor with the populace as well. In 1674 Shadwell altered it very slightly, his "improvements" being mainly in the direction of more operatic features, and this version was to continue until the late nineteenth century as more favored than the original lyrical fantasy of Shakespeare.[14] If Davenant's innovations could be preferred by theatre-goers for two hundred years, it would be folly to treat them lightly. One is not required to

[12] Since the version printed in the Maidment and Logan edition is actually Shadwell's later alteration, for purposes of this study I have used the original Davenant-Dryden version which is published in Montague Summers, *Shakespeare Adaptations* (Boston, 1922). Footnoting for this play will provide Act and Scene number.

[13] Nethercot, p. 402.

[14] For an account of the theatrical success of the Davenant-Dryden and Shadwell texts, see Summers, *Shakespeare Adaptations*, pp. xi-xii, xlix; Maidment and Logan edition of Davenant, V, 397-412.

approve the new additions in order to admit their theatrical impact.[15]

In this new adaptation the most noticeable excision has been the Antonio-Sebastian conspiracy, and for sound reason, since the collaborators seem uninterested in Shakespeare's theme of contrasting the world's evil with the innocence of an island retreat. On the other hand, the most notable additions are to the Miranda plot and the drunken sailor episode. In Shakespeare's version the story of the lovely maiden who has never seen a man composes about one-sixth of the play, during which time it is more marked for its charm than wit. The low comedy provided by Stephano, Trinculo, and Caliban serves to evoke laughter for almost a quarter of the play. This same subplot, though considerably revised, consumes about as much space in the Davenant-Dryden script. But the Miranda story is broadened and lengthened until it occupies almost half the playing time. Obviously these two adapters had little interest in either Shakespeare's high romance or his delicate balancing of age versus youth. Only the comic potentialities inherent in the plot were to attract them.

To balance Miranda's predicament, a handsome youth named Hippolito, who has never seen a woman, is provided. Then in order that Hippolito may not be left matchless once Miranda meets Ferdinand, Miranda is supplied with a younger sister Dorinda, who may be as innocent as her sister regarding the function of men, but certainly more eager to remedy such a shortcoming. As to whether Davenant or Dryden is responsible for these passages, scholars are in disagreement. We do know, because Dryden has informed us, that Hippolito is the invention of Davenant.[16] Beyond that we cannot be sure. One German scholar has even attempted to prove that these episodes and Hippolito owe their origin to Calderon's *En ésta vida todo es verdad y todo mentira.*[17] Not until Harbage's biography of Davenant appeared did anyone

[15] A brief analysis of the adaptation is to be found in Hazelton Spencer, *Shakespeare Improved* (Cambridge, Mass., 1927), pp. 192-204.

[16] John Dryden, Preface to *The Tempest*, in Davenant, V, 414.

[17] Hermann Grimm, "Shakespeare's Sturm in der Bearbeitung von Dryden und Davenant", in *Fünfzehn Essays* (Berlin, 1875), pp. 183-224, quoted in Summers, *Shakespeare Adaptations*, pp. xlix-liii.

note that in 1635, several years before Calderon's play was printed,
Davenant had created in *The Platonic Lovers* a young man,
Gridonell, who had never seen a woman. Dryden's word as to the
invention of Hippolito can surely be accepted. And this Hazelton
Spencer accepts, though he insists that no one but Dryden actually
wrote the comedy, explaining thus, "As we have seen, D'Avenant
was almost a prude where verbal grossness was to be dealt with." [18]
Spencer is taking Davenant too much at his word. Despite his
claim, as a Restoration producer, to purify the theatre, Davenant,
as the student knows only too well, displayed in his earlier comedies no manifestations of a prude. In fact, a close study of the
Gridonell scenes will reveal a dialogue that closely parallels in
quality the "freedoms" which Spencer will attribute only to "one
of the loosest of the English dramatists". In any case we know
from Dryden's Preface that Davenant corrected what the junior
dramatist wrote, and since the play was to be produced in his own
theatre, he obviously approved of the "verbal grossness". Therefore, these scenes can be considered here, in point of comedy, as
belonging to Davenant.

Shakespeare's first act concludes with the luminously tender
scene of Miranda's initial meeting with Ferdinand. This same
episode is postponed in the Davenant-Dryden version until the
audience's curiosity is more than kindled. Substituted instead is a
disarming episode wherein Miranda and her younger sister puzzle
over the purpose of man. Such naiveté in two maidens who are so
obviously ripe for a gallant's plucking must surely have titillated
the blasé fancies of Restoration rakes. Halfway through the second
act Hippolito appears, and after revealing to the audience in his
discussion with Prospero how he happens to have always lived
secluded on the island, he rather vehemently expresses his antipa-
thy to the sex he has never seen. With unconscious irony, he says,

> But let them not provoke me, for I'm sure
> I shall not then forbear them.   (II, ii)

Immediately after he leaves stage, Prospero's two daughters appear, and the old man enters into a similar conversation with
them, warning them of imminent perils:

[18]   Spencer, p. 202.

Mira: But you have told me, Sir, you are a man;
         And yet you are not dreadful.
Pros: Ay, child! but I
         Am a tame man; old men are tame by nature,
         But all the danger lies in a wild young man.
Dori: Do they run wild about the woods?
Pros: No, they are wild within doors, in chambers,
         And in closets.
Dori: But, father, I would stroak them, and make them gentle;
         Then sure they would not hurt me.
Pros: You must not trust them, child: No woman can
         Come near them but she feels a pain, full nine months. (II, ii)

Following such a liberal sprinkling of *double-entendres*, veering
close to but never quite reaching the salacious, the audience is
eager for the first meeting between the sexes. Rather than let his
spectators' interest wane, the playwright at once satisfies it.
Hippolito enters. For a short while the two maidens never venture
more than to peep at him, until finally and fortunately their mutual attraction draws them together. Soon Dorinda, the more for-
ward sister, is holding hands with the youth and exchanging
pleasantries that are certainly racy in their unintended implica-
tions. Particularly is this so in the none-too-subtle use of animal
images. In referring to their mutual need to be kind, not harmful,
Hippolito informs her of his observation:

> . . . . for, when two poisonous creatures,
> Both of the same kind, meet, yet neither dies.
> I've seen two serpents harmless to each other,
> Though they have twined into a mutual knot:
> If we have any venom in us, sure, we cannot be
> More poisonous, when we meet, than serpents are. (II, iii)

After she replies with another immodest allusion, this time to "two
mourning turtles", one keenly anticipates Prospero's paternal
problems.

In the third act this plot turns briefly serious so that Prospero
may discuss the girls' reaction to a male. During this dialogue,
relatively little wit is present. Not until Hippolito learns from
Ferdinand that the emotions he feels are called "love" does the

comedy regain impact. Avidly the audience watches the lad's
enthusiasm, his eagerness to indulge newly-awakened passions
with all and sundry females. Frankly ingenuous in this scene,
Hippolito is very reminiscent of Gridonell in Davenant's earlier
tragicomedy. Likewise, like Gridonell, Miranda is equally innocent of how civilized man pursues his mate, although her behavior
more deeply disturbs Ferdinand. Overly earnest in her wish that
Ferdinand will love Hippolito, she is baffled as to her suitor's apparent coolness to the proposal. Were she to hear his "aside",
crude as it is, she would still be uninformed:

> It is too plain: Like most of her frail sex
> She's false, but has not learned the art to hide it.
> Nature has done her part, she loves variety: –
> Why did I think that any woman could
> Be innocent, because she's young? No, no!
> Their nurses teach them change, when, with two nipples, they
> Divide their liking.   (IV, i)

The complications continue. Dorinda becomes disturbed by
Hippolito's polygamous inclinations and attempts to impress upon
him how unseemly her sister is, even to stating that she wears a
beard like her father. Hippolito, undeterred for his own interests,
supports man's double standard by insisting upon Dorinda's complete fidelity. But there is little agreement. Eventually Ferdinand
and Hippolito fight a duel, despite the latter's ignorance of the
procedure. Hippolito falls and apparently dies. The maidens blame
each other's swain. Prospero arrives, hears the case, and condemns
Ferdinand to death. At such a point, far removed from the Comic
Spirit, the fourth act ends.

In the final act all is resolved, as to be expected, happily, but
not before there are more amusing misunderstandings among the
four lovers, most of them being fairly decent in tone. Then immediately before the curtain falls the playwright panders again to
one's appetite for the indirectly obscene. A live Hippolito having
been returned to Dorinda, and with Miranda's plight to Ferdinand
announced, the two sisters turn their minds to another mental
quandary that is aroused by Prospero's order that they repair to
bed to produce children:

Mira: (to Dorinda) If children come by lying in a bed,
   I wonder you and I had none between us.
Dori: Sister, it was our fault; we meant, like fools,
   To look 'em in the fields, and they, it seems,
   Are only found in beds.
Hip: I am o'er-joyed,
   That I shall have Dorinda in a bed;
   We'll lie all night and day together there,
   And never rise again.
   . . . . (V, ii)

Were a Restoration audience to have had this innocent lovers' plot alone, it might have been sufficient to have amused their elegantly decadent tastes. Much of it is witty, and more of it is slightly indecent. Yet in addition there is a subplot of low comedy which is definitely, according to Dryden, the work of Davenant.[19]

Ingenuous as the characters are in the above plot, the spirit of it is essentially Restoration. In sharp contrast is the pre-Restoration slapstick, entirely wholesome in tone, that features Trinculo, Stephano, Caliban, and company. Trinculo, no longer a jester, is a Boatswain, and thus arrogates to himself a more commanding and insolent role than he heretofore enjoyed. Stephano, once a drunken butler, becomes nothing less than Master of the Ship. Mustacho, a mate, and Ventoso, a mariner, are added to the motley band. Following the shipwreck, all but Trinculo find themselves together, washed ashore on a wild part of the island. Except for a "runlet of brandy" salvaged from the disaster, they are bereft, free to bewail unheard their lost happiness. Memories of their wives, even Ventoso's one-eyed spouse, bring exaggerated lamentations. Disorder reigns. Then Ventoso broaches the subject of forming a government, his hope being to avoid future cannibalism. Immediately enthusiastic, Stephano proclaims himself Duke. His first duty is to settle his cronies' greed for power by appointing both of them viceroys. At this point a drunken Trinculo enters, having floated to safety on a butt of sack. Irked by this new regime, Trinculo refuses to obey its dictum and, therefore, is proclaimed a rebel.

It is not long before Trinculo's rebellion gains momentum.

---

[19] Dryden's Preface to *The Tempest,* in *Davenant,* V, 414.

Pouring wine down the throat of Caliban, a duty belonging to Stephano in the Shakespeare play, he soon has that uncouth monster swearing allegiance. Further still, to prove his good faith, Caliban promises to gain the support of his own sister, Sycorax. This latter product of Davenant's desire to double Shakespeare's comic characters does not appear until the third act. It is just as well. With too much exposure, such a grotesque female might prove more disgusting than diverting. Even Trinculo must suppress his contempt if he is to pursue his goal. With zest he woos her with such fond endearments, absurd when related to their object, as "my dear blobber lips", "my chuck", and "my fair fuss" (III, iii). Overcome with this attention, Caliban's sister capitulates. In fact, so ardent is she that an apprehensive Trinculo must beg her to be less boisterous. Duly considered, it appears that Trinculo's cause will strengthen.

In Act Four, an anxious Stephano decides to undermine the rebel's growing position. To Sycorax, now called Queen Blouze the First by her ambitious spouse, he performs the role of the Biblical serpent:

Syco: But did he tell you so?
Steph: He said you were as ugly as your mother, and that he married you only to get possession of the island.
Syco: My mother's devils fetch him for't!
Steph: And your father's too. Hem! skink about his grace's health again. O if you will but cast an eye of pity upon me –
Syco: I will cast two eyes of pity on thee; I love thee more than haws or blackberries. I have a hoard of wildings in the moss, my brother knows not of 'em; But I'll bring thee where they are.   (IV, iii)

His plan works. Abetted by liquor, in Caliban's case the want of it, a melée erupts. As Trinculo states, "the whole nation is up in arms" (IV, iii). Nevertheless, in spite of the pressing problems disturbing his "state", Trinculo is aware of a yet more irritating issue. Surprising as it sounds to the audience, he is intent not only on suing Sycorax for a separation, but to seek alimony as well. With this touch of civilized domesticity, the farcical antics of this subplot conclude.

Though different in tone and subject from Shakespeare's low comedy, this knockabout farce, more akin to the Elizabethan than the Restoration, never fails to entertain with high amusement. It is no more than fantastic buffoonery, but it does balance well with the ribaldries of the main plot to keep an audience laughing constantly. Proof of its continuing entertainment value is demonstrated by the success of its revival during the summer of 1959 by the Old Vic Company in London, England. Yet Davenant's last effort in adapting Shakespeare has been rewarded frequently with violent abuse from literary bardolaters. Had it not been so theatrically effective, they would never have given it so much thought.

THE MAN'S THE MASTER

One would assume that King Charles II might have favored Davenant's last adaptation, in fact his last dramatic effort, *The Man's the Master*. A reasonably close redaction of Scarron's *Jodelet, ou Le Maître Valet*, in turn an adaptation of *Donde hay agravios no hay zelos* by F. de Rojas,[20] it is a comedy of the Spanish intrigue genre that generally pleased the carefree monarch. As it happened, however, if we can believe Pepys, the king was disappointed when he attended the premiere on March 26, 1668. Nevertheless, *The Man's the Master* was destined to become a popular favorite, being produced as late as 1775.[21]

Beginning with a brief page or two of dialogue indebted to Scarron's *L'héritier Ridicule* [22] Davenant then follows the Jodelet farce scene by scene. The main plot is still the same. Don John, about to pay his respects to the lovely Isabella whom he has affianced without having seen, is informed by his insolent valet, Jodelet, that the latter's picture has been submitted, mistakenly to be sure, to the lady. At first furious, the Don is soon calmed by

---

[20]   Harbage, *Sir William Davenant, Poet Venturer 1606-1668*, p. 256.
[21]   Harbage, p. 257.
[22]   A helpful dissertation on the methods of adaptation found in *The Man's the Master* is Max Schmerbach, *Das Verhältnis von Davenant's "The Man's the Master" zu Scarron's "Jodelet, Ou le Maître Valet"* (Halle-Wittenberg, 1899).

seeing the hurried descent from his betrothed's balcony of a cavalier. Instantly he determines to exchange identities with Jodelet so that he can better reconnoiter the household. Don John is unaware that the escaping cavalier, now paying his attentions to Isabella, is the same man who caused the seduction and eventual flight of his own sister Lucilla as well as the death of his brother, both crimes which necessitate his revenge. Nor does Don John know that Lucilla is presently taking sanctuary under the kind guidance of Isabella's father, Don Ferdinand. Although it is not long before Don Ferdinand surmises the various relationships, except for the exchanged identities, it is not until numerous complications evolve that the other characters become aware of the proximity of those to whom they are so closely connected. Eventually, following much anxiety caused by the fake Don John's unseemly attitude and the heroine's fear that she is degrading herself by falling in love with a servant, actually the disguised Don John, the truth comes out. What is comic in these disguises and deceptions belongs to Scarron. Davenant merely appropriates them. But Davenant does make alterations and he even adds a couple of characters, all of which are important to the comic effect of the whole. As in his reworking of the Sganarelle farce, Davenant has curtailed the dialogue. Regarding this, one recalls a remark Davenant made in *The Playhouse to be Let:*

> The French convey their arguments too much
> In dialogue; their speeches are too long.   (IV, 29)

No matter what he thought of the Frenchman's loquacity, his purpose in shortening the speeches in the two plays differs. In the previous comedy he was forced to write a one-acter that could join four other acts in one evening's entertainment. Thus he eliminated almost anything that was not directly pertinent to the development of plot. In *The Man's the Master*, although similar pruning occurs occasionally,[23] there is less need to tighten the play. But there is a need to intensify the dramatic effect of much of the

---

[23] For example see Isabelle's long speech (III, iv) in Scarron, *Théâtre Complet*, with biography by Edouard Fournier (Paris, 1879), p. 281, and Davenant's equivalent in V, 45-46, noting the difference in ironic effect.

dialogue. Too often Scarron's characters in conversation with another will speak at tedious length without interruption. In the English comic theatre where audiences are more impatient of extended talk for the sake of talk alone, such long speeches have never been welcomed. In at least five important instances (V; 17, 28, 30, 44, 83), Davenant breaks up the long addresses characteristic of Scarron by inserting brief statements of the other character present. Thus he forestalls a monotony of dramatic delivery and increases the sense of human conflict in action. This is particularly effective in the treatment of Jodelet, for he is more comical when seen in contact with others. Jodelet needs company in order to display through character contrast his affectionate absurdities. In isolation he becomes merely tiresome. Beyond doubt, these alterations alone, minor as they may appear, contribute considerably to the English taste in comedy.

Minor also are the differences noted in the characterization of Jodelet. In the main they consist of a few extra lines of dialogue, inserted occasionally, that not only pad the part, but in addition extend the amusing aspects of Jodelet's eccentricities. In the first scene of Scarron's play, when Don Juan urges Jodelet to enquire of a stranger the whereabouts of Don Ferdinand's house, the servant is characteristically timid:

D. Juan: Paix là! je vois quelqu'un qui saura bien peut-être
               Où loge don Fernand: va le joindre.
Jodelet: Mon maître!
D. Juan: Que veux-tu? parle bas.
Jodelet: Peut-être il n'en sait rien. (I, i)

In Davenant this last utterance is replaced by,

               Perhaps he'll expect a reward if he tells us.
               In Madrid you must hold out your money if you do but ask
                  what's a clock.   (V, 18)

For subtlety, Scarron betters his successor. Yet in Davenant's substitute, the broad farcical effects for which he strove are most happily evident. It is this same goal of breadth rather than depth in comedy that determines a few added lines to the conclusion of Act One, an addition that does much to whet our appetite for the antics to follow. Following their switch in identities, Jodelet, his boldness bolstered by his new position, warns his master:

. . . .
Wait close upon Don Jodelet thy master;
And thou mayst be my carver, or my taster,
If thou dost fetch me girls, and watch, and trudge well,
Thou shalt have food, if not, thou shalt have cudgel. (V, 22)

Jodelet's first meeting with the luckless Isabella reveals more impertinence, excessive gallantry, and more ridiculous bravado in the additional dialogue provided:

Jodelet: My heart beats too much at sight of my mistress. If I faint with love be sure to hold me up.

D. John: I shall, sir!

Jodelet: Lady, you say nothing: but I'm glad you are silent, for, if you should shew as much wit as you do beauty, I were a dead man. Jodelet!

D. John: Sir!

Jodelet: To drive away the sorrows of love, I prithee break a jeast or two, or tell my mistress some of mine to cure her melancholy.

Isabella: My father has made a rare choice. This extraordinary fool is only fit for Christmas.

Jodelet: Don Ferdinand, do you always serve for a skreen to your daughter?

D. John: (aside) Unlucky rogue! what devil taught thee to ask that?

D. Lewis: That question is not very civil.

Jodelet: Those that are angry may shew their teeth; but let them be sure that they be sharp.

D. Lewis: Sir, no man will doubt yours.

Jodelet: Those who dare doubt mine may meet me – at diner; and after dinner may walk a turn in the field. It may be wholesome for some, but for others it may prove dangerous.

(V, 37)

Considering this unlikely demeanor from a suitor, is it any wonder that Isabella is baffled by her father's choice? Again, it is just such a crude compliment made by Jodelet that would shock even the most weathered socialite:

. . . . Lady you laugh scurvily! you laugh like a monkey that has stol'n cherries; he, he, he, he! (V, 38)

Later, when Jodelet asks his servant to court Isabella for him, Davenant provides a novel reason that adds to the imposter's clownish qualities:

Sirrah, I say advance! and court her handsomely, whilst I go to the gate, and consult with the porter how to scatter a little gold amongst the servants, to shew my bounty and make friends. (V, 50)

It is always amusing to see an exaggerated display of generosity in a person not sincerely inclined, and this Davenant exploits to comic advantage.

But it is Jodelet's cowardice that is so characteristic of Scarron's creation. Davenant wisely keeps this aspect and exaggerates it. Years before, when he wrote *The Siege*, he had good practise in creating a swaggering poltroon. This apprenticeship stands him in good stead. Throughout the famous duel scene Davenant continually inserts more cryptic remarks, all designed to drain what humor is possible in the situation of a bragging coward's bluff being called. And then to finish the play Davenant adds a speech that is a triumph. Brightly it reveals that our flirtatious boaster has not yet learned his lesson:

> . . . . That's fine i' faith,
> Sweet lady; but 'twill not do. Restore
> It to me or be sure you never walk
> Abroad alone after the sun is set.
> Don Jodelet is such a furious spark
> As will have satisfaction in the dark. (V, 104)

In this portrait of Jodelet, his folly is one that no amount of experience can correct. This refusal to conform we enjoy.

Notwithstanding Davenant's comic touches in depicting Jodelet, the success of that superb creation belongs essentially to Scarron. There is little an adapter can do to improve upon what is near perfection. Thus, if Davenant's own talents are to be seriously taxed, new characters must be offered. This Davenant has done. Knowing how English audiences, unlike the French, have a peculiar affinity for witnessing the affairs of household servants when presented mirthfully, he emphasizes the liveliness of backstairs behavior.

Bettris, Isabella's maid, has her counterpart in Scarron's Beatrix, the lady's maid who involves herself, whether solicited or not, in her mistress' private affairs. And Stephano, Don Louis' valet, is the equivalent of Scarron's Etienne. Nevertheless, Scarron would scarcely recognize his servants. Though he suggested an impertinent Beatrix, he never realized the earthy interest that Davenant drew. Bettris is still the schemer, but now she schemes as much, if not more, in her own interests. The stereotyped coquette, still she always plays safe:

Bettris: Retire to the garret over that chamber where I must hide your master, and there you must lye close.

Stephano: I should lye closer if you were with me.

Bettris: Certainly you men are very cold creatures: you are always wishing for something to keep you warm.

Stephano: Ah, Bettris! a garret without a chimney is a cold habitation. But if you were near me –

Bettris: I know but one hoop in the world can bind us close together.

Stephano: What do you mean?

Bettris: A wedding ring. (V, 40-41)

Bettris is obviously a woman with whom a male may take more verbal liberties than Beatrix would have accepted. In answer to Bettris' question, "O sir, is it you?" Stephano replies, "None but a maid who loves to meet men in the dark would ask that question with her eyes open." Noting that his speech replaces Etienne's, "Non, c'est le grand Mogol", we note that in being transplanted she displays far less propriety of conduct than the French drama would have found acceptable in depicting a servant.

By far the funniest of all these retainers, however, is Sancho, Davenant's own creation. Though his colleagues are voluble, always eager to banter frank quips and jests, he appears remarkably vivid through an unwillingness to disturb his vocal cords unduly. At the very beginning of the play, the fugitive Lucilla and her maid Laura acquaint us with this curious "humor". It is night and they are searching for Don Ferdinand's house when Sancho appears with a lantern:

Lucilla: What is he?

Laura: 'Tis Sancho, Don Ferdinando's steward! he was my sworn brother over a posset; he is, by the length of his beard and the heat of his constitution, a very goat.

Lucilla: For heaven's sake lose no time!

Laura: You need not fear his loss of time; I use to call him by brother Brevity; he is so thrifty of his speech, that his tongue does seldom allow his thoughts above two words to express them.

Sancho: Laura!

Laura: Are not you my brother Sancho?

Sancho: I am.

Laura: Have you contriv'd a way to conceal my lady in your master's house?

Sancho: Yes.

Laura: Can you admit her now?

Sancho: No.

Laura: May it be to-morrow?

Sancho: It may.

Laura: I'll attend you in the morning.

Sancho: Do.

Laura: Pray name the hour.

Sancho: Nine.

Laura: My mistress is very sensible of your care, and would know if I may have leave to give you this gold?

Sancho: You may.

Laura: I hope you hate not me, nor the present.

Sancho: Neither.

Laura: Are we both acceptable?

Sancho: Both.   (He looks on the gold.)

Laura: 'Tis very gold! and Signior Sancho you shall find me to be as true metal as it.

Sancho: I'll try. –   (Offers to kiss her.)

Laura: Not so soon, good Signior Sancho. Bring me to the wedding night, and then try, if, like gold, I can endur the touch.

Sancho: Humph!

Laura: Lovers may pretend to have true metal, but marriage is the touch-stone.

Sancho: Of fools.   (Aside)

Laura: Hands off, good Signior Sancho. You want sleep. Good night! Pray let me go!

Sancho: Pass!   (V, 12-13)

From the above colloquy it is obvious that Sancho does have definite instincts, even though the instinct to speak is not one of them.

It is this latter failing that provokes the ire of Don John in a scene of Davenant's invention, causing him to say, "This laconic fool makes brevity ridiculous" (V, 32). On the other hand, in this same scene, Jodelet voices his appreciation of such silent behavior. Obviously it gives him more opportunity to hear his own bombastic nothings. It is this gift of being a foil to a fool that adds to Sancho's value in this scene, since his terse queries inspire Jodelet to rave about his own magnanimity, in this case an extraordinary kindness of fleas.

Two of the most amusing new episodes in this adaptation are inspired by Sancho's gluttony. His appetite for sack-posset demands a scene in which all the servants are gathered for a midnight feast. While others stir, Sancho eats. According to the stage directions he "slobbers his beard", and a little later "he takes a huge knife out of his pocket, scrapes the posset off from his beard, and then eats it" (V, 66-67). To be sure, the comedy of this scene is centered around Jodelet, whose own hungry stomach draws him to the servants' revel, much to the disgust of the disguised Don Juan. But were it not for Sancho's original desire for the food, the playwright would have had to discover another means of allowing Jodelet such a farcical display of ill-breeding. A later scene, however, exists solely for Sancho. It, too, results from his inordinate fondness for food. After promising him a marvellous collation of hams, cabbage leaves, pistachoes, mussels, roasted chestnuts, and ragouts strewed over with saltpeter and Jamaica pepper, the other servants persuade him to be blindfolded. Then turning him in a circle they dance about, kicking him as they sing. The ignominy of this forced exercise being over, the eager Sancho waits for his collation. There is none:

Bettris: We did this to save you a labour; for when no crumbs can fall upon your beard you need not brush it.
Sancho: I could eat.
Laura: What?
Sancho: Thee. (V, 91)

Furious at this betrayal Sancho runs off stage, not to appear again until the happy conclusion when Don Ferdinand promises feasts. True to his "humor" to the end, broadly portrayed, Sancho is representative of Davenant's intention in translating Scarron's comedy. Anything that was nonsensical, foolish, even tasteless in the original, Davenant appropriated should it be worthy of laughter. And to it he added his own generous portions of the ridiculous. As a result he produced a romp that is closer to "horseplay" than anything he had so far written. The fact that it became so popular witnesses how well Davenant the producer gauged his audience's theatrical tastes.

A thoughtful consideration of all his translations and adaptations will emphasize how much Davenant the producer supplanted Davenant the playwright. It is incorrect to label the various excrescences of these versions as a sign of his waning powers. To be sure such an admission warrants some acceptance. But it was his thoughtful concern for his ledger that really determined the approach he took. To be sure he could never emulate the elegance of repartee and skill of plotting that is common to the great Restoration playwrights. But then those comedies we revere today were not the most favored in their own age. Restoration audiences are overly flattered by our thinking so. The more representative fare is closer to the kind of comedy Davenant here presents.

VI

CONCLUSION

Though the Comic Spirit operates on certain permanent principles, like all else in this world it is subject to the fluctuations of fashion. Tastes alter as man passes from one social stratum to another; they alter again as one decade gives way to a new one; and with these changes in taste, that which a man finds laughable alters too. To adjust with a minimum of frustration to this ever-constant change requires a man of flexible and unprejudiced intellect. To encompass the varieties of taste in comedy that was characteristic of seventeenth-century audiences required Davenant. Throughout his forty-year career, which spanned the reigns of three kings and the administrations of two dictators, Davenant was often required to meet varieties of fashion in comic drama. That he was always successful, one would never affirm. That he was always bold in meeting the challenge, one could never deny. And in doing so Davenant was the most comprehensive comic dramatist in his age.

It would be folly to contend that any one type of comedy is basic to his drama. One might be tempted to extol the comedy of humors as being of fundamental interest to this playwright, for aspects of it appear throughout all his work. From his early trage-dy, *The Cruel Brother*, with its concern for the comic gulls, Borachio and Lothario, until the appearance of a taciturn Sancho in *The Man's the Master*, there is scarcely a drama in which a "humor" is absent. Sometimes they are soldiers or sailors, at other times they are supercilious courtiers or wittily malign bravos, but always they exist in that comic realm where one aspect of man's mental makeup is exaggerated in order to amuse. Perhaps the amusement evoked is satirical, or it might be farcical; at its best both satire and farce will blend in such a buffoon as Gridonell, the youth who knows so little about woman that he is determined to learn all. Yet Davenant was not content to ape only the comedy Jonson perfected. Other tastes were being expressed, and he was quick to follow them.

Though the comedy of manners would not receive first rank for at least three more decades, Davenant was aware as early as *The Just Italian* of certain characteristics that it was to perfect later. When Alteza bargains with her husband, she foreshadows a type of female that would eventually dominate the theatrical scene. To be sure, Alteza's plight is akin to that of several stage heroines already depicted, notably Petruchio's Katharina in Shakespeare's rowdy comedy, although the resemblance to the latter female is not complete. Alteza is an independent, self-assured woman, whereas Katharina is merely a stubborn shrew. Alteza is convinced of her own value as an individual who is entitled to equal rights with her husband, and she insists on having such rights recognized. In arguing with her spouse, she points the way to the justly-revered Millamant-Mirabell bargaining scene in Congreve's come, dy. Closer still to the Restoration ideal in their wittiness of repartee are the two brilliant ladies who dominate Davenant's two full-length comedies, Lady Ample in *The Wits* and Lady Loveright in *News from Plymouth*. Their male counterpart is best exemplified in Androlio, the cheerfully cynical roué of *The Distresses*, who, like Restoration rakes, poses a type of masculine ideal that men, and their foolish sisters, were long to admire. In characterization, concern for social form, and tone, there are in these comedies and tragicomedies frequent reminders of the comedy of manners which Davenant, both as playwright and producer, helped to inaugurate.

A brief glance at *The Just Italian, The Distresses*, and *The Rivals* reveals the author's affection for the comedy of intrigue. Even his devotion to the subplot of *The Man's the Master*, that is the emphasis on servants' wild pranks backstairs, not present in the Scarron original, is allied to the Spanish comedy of intrigue where servants' boisterous behavior is generally a delightful diversion from the complexities of the main plot. As in the comedies of humors and manners, "intrigue" elements in these dramas of Davenant bespeak the playwright's familiarity with his spectators' interests.

Though he was usually a follower of the dramatic trends in his time, occasionally Davenant would attempt to lead. Students of his career recognize this courage in his introducing of heroic tragedy and in new methods of staging a play. One such innovation appeared in his dramatization of comedy. With his burlesque of the Antony and Cleopatra legend, he introduced to the Restoration theatre a genre of comic writing that would continue to please the reader and spectator alike. Unfortunately, he never continued in this mode. His talents were diverted elsewhere, namely in managing a company of actors. But he made the beginning, and its reception justified the attempt.

In addition to his talent for recognizing and practising the various comic modes of seventeenth-century drama, Davenant was particularly gifted with a keen eye for the topical. When the love and honor theme was popular, he bravely portrayed it in order to please his audience and his queen. He may not have been in sympathy with its excesses, as numerous examples in *The Platonick Lovers* would suggest, but he was always adroit enough not to alienate his patrons. At another time, when it became obvious that jokes at a Frenchman's expense would be favored, he wrote an extended dialogue between a Londoner and a Parisian that illustrates mirthfully the difference between the two capital cities and their inhabitants. Later, in his adaptations, similarly unkind jibes occasionally appear, but none was so extended as the pseudo-French dialect used throughout his translation of Molière's *Sganarelle ou le Cocu Imaginaire*.

Usually this topical interest is displayed in the interest of satire. Occasionally farce is the goal, as in the subplot of *The Wits* and *News from Plymouth*, but more often the playwright's intention is to correct through indirect criticism. In *Albovine*, his first play, the comic satire depicted in Grimold, the virulent-tongued social commentator, is in the sardonic vein that is so characteristic of much Jacobean drama, both comedy and tragedy. Later, with the Caroline period well advanced, Davenant's satire instructs in a less vicious manner. The court parasites in *The Fair Favourite*, parading about, gossiping, and picking teeth, are not kindly presented, to be sure, but the tone of their depiction is a mocking raillery that leaves no doubt in the spectator's mind as to how ridiculously humorous they are. Similar is the mild satire on debauched Cavaliers to be found in Androlio, a debauchée without peer in *The Distresses*. When he wants to, as in his affectionate portrayal of Lucy's love for Young Pallatine in *The Wits*, Davenant can be so gentle in his handling of the Comic Spirit as to approximate the sentimental comedy of the next century. And throughout all his plays, even in the Restoration years, when he pretended to be purifying the stage, he always has a healthy masculine appreciation for the *double-entendre* and the bawdy joke. Never squeamish, neither was he interested in the perverse. Though undeniably ribald at times, as in the Basco episode of *Love and Honour*, or even archly witty, yet such humor always results from a naturally lusty enjoyment of the sexual process. Rarely does it offend.

Satire usually inspires Davenant's interest in the topical to comprehend many minor details of daily existence, which, in turn, produce the charming local color so noticeable in many of these comic scenes. Such are his comments on warfare to be found in *The Wits* and in *The Siege*. Bogus spiritual tracts, local constabulary, pedagogues and philosophers, Jesuits and jailors, all receive the brunt of Davenant's broadsides. There was little that was sacred to this skeptical realist, and when he found that which appeared to be revered, be it fad, philosophy, or routine idea, he delighted in levying his satirical sallies.

Wonderful as is Davenant's treatment of local color, one recognizes in it an important reason why his dramatic treatment of comedy has not been carefully evaluated. Davenant's artistry was too concerned with the local, the topical, the transitory. And, as well, his comedy is usually external, concerned with the physical rather than the mental qualities of comedy. Combine these two features, topicality and external comedy, and one produces comedy that has only an ephemeral value for an audience. To be great comedy, universality must be present, a sense that the events and the characters portrayed are related to the world of ordinary life that supersedes any one particular time in history. The closest Davenant comes to this kind of universality is *The Wits*, an excellent comedy with enough inward appeal to deserve recognition along with the best written in the seventeenth century. On other occasions, as in the subplot of *The Siege*, he suggests a talent for creating such universality, but the suggestion is not fulfilled.

Davenant, in his early years, sought fame. During the middle years, his interests turned away from the theatre. In his senior years, the tasks of a producer became his passion. Governed by such varying externalities, he was never to take pains in perfecting his plays. He compromised with his art for success, and, on occasion, his compromises failed to bring him even that. Thus, for all his gifts in writing comedy, his verbal dexterity, his feeling for the absurd, his understanding of homely realities, he will always be overshadowed by an Etherege or a Congreve. These more deft dramatists were more restricted in their interests, surely, but their interests they polished. Davenant's interests, on the other hand, were more diverse than any of his contemporaries. They touched upon all aspects of comedy known to his time. For the student interested in meeting the many faces of the Comic Spirit in that complex age, there is no playwright more rewarding in his comprehensiveness of treatment than Sir William Davenant.

BIBLIOGRAPHY

A. PRIMARY SOURCES

1. *Studies of plays by Davenant*

Davenant, William, *The Dramatic Works of Sir William D'Avenant, with Prefatory Memoir and Notes*, edd. J. Maidment and W. H. Logan, 5 vols. (Edinburgh-London, 1872-74).
Summers, Montague, *Shakespeare Adaptations* (Boston, 1922).

2. *Studies of writings which influenced Davenant or were influenced by him*

Beaumont, Thomas and Fletcher, John, *The Works of Beaumont and Fletcher*, ed. A. R. Waller, 10 vols. (Cambridge, 1905-12).
Brome, Richard, *The Dramatic Works of Richard Brome*, 3 vols. (London, 1873).
Cervantes, *The Ingenious Gentleman Don Quixote de la Mancha*, trans. Samuel Putnam, 2 vols. (New York, 1949).
Congreve, William, *The Works of Congreve*, ed. F. W. Bateson (London, 1930).
Dekker, Thomas, *The Dramatic Works of Thomas Dekker*, ed. Fredson Bowers, 3 vols. (Cambridge, 1953-58).
Etherege, Sir George, *The Dramatic Works of Sir George Etherege*, ed. H. F. B. Brett-Smith, 2 vols. (Oxford, 1925).
Farquhar, George, *The Complete Works of George Farquhar*, ed. Charles Stonehilly, 2 vols. (Bloomsbury, 1930).
Glapthorne, Henry, *The Plays and Poems of Henry Glapthorne*, 2 vols. (London, 1874).
Jonson, Ben, *The Complete Plays of Ben Jonson*, with Introduction by Felix E. Schelling, 12 vols. (London, 1925-35).
Marston, John, *The Works of John Marston*, ed. A. H. Bullen, 3 vols. (London, 1887).

Middleton, Thomas, *The Works of Thomas Middleton*, ed. A. H. Bullen, 8 vols. (Boston, 1885-86).

Molière, J. B. P., *Œuvres de Molière*, II, ed. Eugene Despois (Paris, 1875).

Scarron, Paul, *Théâtre Complet*, with biography by Edouard Fournier (Paris, 1879).

Shirley, James, *The Dramatic Works and Poems of James Shirley*, ed. William Gifford, 6 vols. (London, 1833).

Vanbrugh, Sir John, *The Complete Works of Sir John Vanbrugh*, ed. Bonamy Dobrée, 4 vols. (Bloomsbury, 1927-28).

Wycherley, William, *The Complete Works of William Wycherley*, ed. Montague Summers, 4 vols. (Soho, 1924).

3. Studies on theory of comedy

Aristotle, *Aristotle on the Art of Poetry*, ed. Lane Cooper (New York, 1913).

Aristotle, *The Rhetoric of Aristotle*, trans. J. E. C. Welldon (London, 1886).

Bergson, Henri, *Laughter; an Essay on the Meaning of the Comic*, auth. trans. Cloudsley Brereton and Fred Rothwell (New York, 1912).

Hobbes, Thomas, *The English Works of Thomas Hobbes of Malmesbury* (London, 1840).

Kant, Emmanuel, *Kant's Critique of Aesthetic Judgment*, trans. James Creed Meredith (Oxford, 1911).

Meredith, George, *An Essay on Comedy and the Uses of the Comic Spirit*, ed. Cooper (New York, 1918).

Plato, *Philebus and Epinomis*, trans. A. E. Taylor (London, 1956).

Walpole, Horace, *The Letters of Horace Walpole Fourth Earl of Oxford*, IX, ed. Mrs. Paget Toynbee (Oxford, 1904).

B. SECONDARY SOURCES

1. Of specific value to this study

Acheson, Arthur, *Shakespeare's Sonnet Story 1592-1598* (London, 1922).

Aubrey, John, *Aubrey's Brief Lives*, ed. Oliver Lawson Dick (London, 1950).

Clinton-Baddeley, Victor Clinton, *The Burlesque Tradition in the English Theatre after 1660* (London, 1952).

Downes, John, *Roscius Anglicanus*, ed. Montague Summers (London, no date).

Evelyn, John, *The Diary of John Evelyn, Esq., F.R.S. from 1641 to 1705-6*, ed. William Bray (London, no date).

Gaw, Allison, "Tuke's *Adventures of Five Hours*, in Relation to the 'Spanish Plot' and to John Dryden", in *Studies in English Drama*, ed. Allison Gaw (Baltimore, 1917).

Harbage, Alfred, *Sir William Davenant, Poet Venturer 1606-1668* (Philadelphia, 1935).

Herbert, Sir Henry, *The Dramatic Records of Sir Henry Herbert, Master of the Revels, 1623-1673*, ed. Joseph Quincy Adams (New Haven, 1917).

Hughes, Leo, *A Century of English Farce* (Princeton, 1956).

Nethercot, Arthur, *Sir William D'Avenant, Poet Laureate and Playwright-Manager* (Chicago, 1938).

Palmer, John Leslie, *The Comedy of Manners* (London, 1913).

Schelling, Felix, *Elizabethan Drama 1558-1642*, I (Boston, 1908).

Schmerbach, Max, *Das Verhältnis von Davenant's "The Man's the Master" zu Scarron's "Jodelet, Ou le Maître Valet"*, dissertation (Halle-Wittenberg, 1899).

Scott, Sir Walter, "Life of John Dryden", in *The Works of John Dryden*, I (London, 1808).

Smith, Dale Farnswroth, *Plays About the Theatre in England from The Rehearsal in 1671 to the Licensing Act in 1737* (New York, 1936).

Souers, Philip Webster, *The Matchless Orinda* (Cambridge, Mass., 1931).

Spencer, Hazelton, *Shakespeare Improved* (Cambridge, Mass., 1927).

Spingarn, Joel E. (ed.), *Critical Essays of the Seventeenth Century* (Oxford, 1908-1909).

Summers, Montague, "Introduction" to Sir Samuel Tuke's *The Adventures of Five Hours*, ed. H. Van Thal (London, no date).

Summers, Montague, *The Playhouse of Pepys* (London, 1935).

Williams, J. D. E., *Sir William Davenant's Relation to Shakespeare*, dissertation (Strassburg, 1905).

2. Of general interest to this study

Boswell, Eleanore, *The Restoration Court Stage 1660-1702* (Cambridge, Mass., 1932).

Cazamian, Louis, *The Development of English Humor, Parts I and II* (Durham, 1952).

Dobrée, Bonamy, *Restoration Comedy 1660-1720* (Oxford, 1924).

Feibleman, J., *In Praise of Comedy* (New York, 1939).

Forsythe, Robert Stanley, *The Relation of Shirley's Plays to the Elizabethan Drama* (New York, 1914).

Fujimura, Thomas H., *The Restoration Comedy of Wit* (Princeton, 1952).

Greig, J. Y. T., *The Psychology of Laughter and Comedy* (New York, 1923).

Hotson, Leslie, *The Commonwealth and Restoration Stage* (Cambridge, Mass., 1928).

Kronenberger, Louis, *The Thread of Laughter* (New York, 1952).

Krutch, Joseph Wood, *Comedy and Conscience after the Restoration* (New York, 1924).

Ludovici, Anthony M., *The Secret of Laughter* (London, 1932).

Lynch, Kathleen M., *The Social Mode of Restoration Comedy* (New York, 1926).

Nason, Arthur H., *James Shirley, Dramatist* (New York, 1915).

Parlin, Hanson T., *A Study in Shirley's Comedies of London Life*, dissertation University of Pennsylvania (1914).

Perry, Henry Ten Eyck, *The Comic Spirit in Restoration Drama* (New Haven, 1925).

Perry, Henry Ten Eyck, *Masters of Dramatic Comedy and their Social Themes* (Cambridge, Mass., 1939).

Smith, John Harrington, *The Gay Couple in Restoration Comedy* (Cambridge, Mass., 1948).

Smith, Willard, *The Nature of Comedy* (Boston, 1930).

Sprague, A. C., *Beaumont and Fletcher on the Restoration Stage* (Cambridge, Mass., 1926).

Stiefel, Arthur Ludwig, "Die Nachahmung spanischer Komödien in England unter den ersten Stuarts", *Romanische Forschungen*, V(Erlangen, 1890).

Underwood, Dale, *Etherege and the Seventeenth Century Comedy of Manners* (New Haven, 1957).

Wilcox, John, *The Relation of Molière to Restoration Comedy* (New York, 1938).

Wilson, John Harold, *The Influence of Beaumont and Fletcher on Restoration Drama* (Columbus, Ohio, 1928).

Winslow, Ola Elizabeth, *Low Comedy as a Structural Element in English Drama from the Beginnings to 1642* (Menasha, Wisc., 1926).